S0-DXC-803

NATIONAL COOPERATIVE FREIGHT RESEARCH PROGRAM

NCFRP REPORT 9

Guidance for Developing a Freight Transportation Data Architecture

Cesar Quiroga
Nicholas Koncz
Edgar Kraus
Juan Villa
Jeffery Warner
Yingfeng Li
David Winterich
TEXAS TRANSPORTATION INSTITUTE
THE TEXAS A&M UNIVERSITY SYSTEM
College Station, TX

Todd Trego
Dunwoody, GA

Jeffrey Short
AMERICAN TRANSPORTATION RESEARCH INSTITUTE
Arlington, VA

Elizabeth Ogard
PRIME FOCUS, LLC
DePere, WI

Subscriber Categories
Data and Information Technology • Economics • Freight Transportation • Marine Transportation • Motor Carriers
Planning and Forecasting • Railroads

Research sponsored by the Research and Innovative Technology Administration

TRANSPORTATION RESEARCH BOARD

WASHINGTON, D.C.
2011
www.TRB.org

NATIONAL COOPERATIVE FREIGHT RESEARCH PROGRAM

America's freight transportation system makes critical contributions to the nation's economy, security, and quality of life. The freight transportation system in the United States is a complex, decentralized, and dynamic network of private and public entities, involving all modes of transportation—trucking, rail, waterways, air, and pipelines. In recent years, the demand for freight transportation service has been increasing fueled by growth in international trade; however, bottlenecks or congestion points in the system are exposing the inadequacies of current infrastructure and operations to meet the growing demand for freight. Strategic operational and investment decisions by governments at all levels will be necessary to maintain freight system performance, and will in turn require sound technical guidance based on research.

The National Cooperative Freight Research Program (NCFRP) is a cooperative research program sponsored by the Research and Innovative Technology Administration (RITA) under Grant No. DTOS59-06-G-00039 and administered by the Transportation Research Board (TRB). The program was authorized in 2005 with the passage of the Safe, Accountable, Flexible, Efficient Transportation Equity Act: A Legacy for Users (SAFETEA-LU). On September 6, 2006, a contract to begin work was executed between RITA and The National Academies. The NCFRP will carry out applied research on problems facing the freight industry that are not being adequately addressed by existing research programs.

Program guidance is provided by an Oversight Committee comprised of a representative cross section of freight stakeholders appointed by the National Research Council of The National Academies. The NCFRP Oversight Committee meets annually to formulate the research program by identifying the highest priority projects and defining funding levels and expected products. Research problem statements recommending research needs for consideration by the Oversight Committee are solicited annually, but may be submitted to TRB at any time. Each selected project is assigned to a panel, appointed by TRB, which provides technical guidance and counsel throughout the life of the project. Heavy emphasis is placed on including members representing the intended users of the research products.

The NCFRP will produce a series of research reports and other products such as guidebooks for practitioners. Primary emphasis will be placed on disseminating NCFRP results to the intended end-users of the research: freight shippers and carriers, service providers, suppliers, and public officials.

NCFRP REPORT 9

Project NCFRP-12
ISSN 1947-5659
ISBN 978-0-309-15523-6
Library of Congress Control Number 2010941126

© 2011 National Academy of Sciences. All rights reserved.

Published reports of the

NATIONAL COOPERATIVE FREIGHT RESEARCH PROGRAM

are available from:

Transportation Research Board
Business Office
500 Fifth Street, NW
Washington, DC 20001

and can be ordered through the Internet at:

http://www.national-academies.org/trb/bookstore

Printed in the United States of America

THE NATIONAL ACADEMIES
Advisers to the Nation on Science, Engineering, and Medicine

The **National Academy of Sciences** is a private, nonprofit, self-perpetuating society of distinguished scholars engaged in scientific and engineering research, dedicated to the furtherance of science and technology and to their use for the general welfare. On the authority of the charter granted to it by the Congress in 1863, the Academy has a mandate that requires it to advise the federal government on scientific and technical matters. Dr. Ralph J. Cicerone is president of the National Academy of Sciences.

The **National Academy of Engineering** was established in 1964, under the charter of the National Academy of Sciences, as a parallel organization of outstanding engineers. It is autonomous in its administration and in the selection of its members, sharing with the National Academy of Sciences the responsibility for advising the federal government. The National Academy of Engineering also sponsors engineering programs aimed at meeting national needs, encourages education and research, and recognizes the superior achievements of engineers. Dr. Charles M. Vest is president of the National Academy of Engineering.

The **Institute of Medicine** was established in 1970 by the National Academy of Sciences to secure the services of eminent members of appropriate professions in the examination of policy matters pertaining to the health of the public. The Institute acts under the responsibility given to the National Academy of Sciences by its congressional charter to be an adviser to the federal government and, on its own initiative, to identify issues of medical care, research, and education. Dr. Harvey V. Fineberg is president of the Institute of Medicine.

The **National Research Council** was organized by the National Academy of Sciences in 1916 to associate the broad community of science and technology with the Academy's purposes of furthering knowledge and advising the federal government. Functioning in accordance with general policies determined by the Academy, the Council has become the principal operating agency of both the National Academy of Sciences and the National Academy of Engineering in providing services to the government, the public, and the scientific and engineering communities. The Council is administered jointly by both the Academies and the Institute of Medicine. Dr. Ralph J. Cicerone and Dr. Charles M. Vest are chair and vice chair, respectively, of the National Research Council.

The **Transportation Research Board** is one of six major divisions of the National Research Council. The mission of the Transportation Research Board is to provide leadership in transportation innovation and progress through research and information exchange, conducted within a setting that is objective, interdisciplinary, and multimodal. The Board's varied activities annually engage about 7,000 engineers, scientists, and other transportation researchers and practitioners from the public and private sectors and academia, all of whom contribute their expertise in the public interest. The program is supported by state transportation departments, federal agencies including the component administrations of the U.S. Department of Transportation, and other organizations and individuals interested in the development of transportation. **www.TRB.org**

www.national-academies.org

COOPERATIVE RESEARCH PROGRAMS

AUTHOR ACKNOWLEDGMENTS

The research reported herein was performed under NCFRP Project 12 by the Texas Transportation Institute (TTI), Texas A&M University System, in collaboration with the American Transportation Research Institute (ATRI), and Prime Focus LLC. TTI was the prime contractor for this study, with the Texas A&M Research Foundation serving as Fiscal Administrator.

Cesar Quiroga, research engineer at TTI, was the principal investigator. The other authors of this report are Nicholas Koncz, assistant research scientist at TTI; Edgar Kraus, associate research engineer at TTI; Juan Villa, research scientist at TTI; Jeffery Warner, associate transportation researcher at TTI; Yingfeng Li, assistant research scientist at TTI; David Winterich, research associate at TTI; Todd Trego, senior research associate; Jeffrey Short, senior research associate at ATRI; and Elizabeth Ogard, president at Prime Focus LLC.

FOREWORD

By William C. Rogers
Staff Officer
Transportation Research Board

NCFRP Report 9: Guidance for Developing a Freight Transportation Data Architecture presents the requirements and specifications for a national freight data architecture to link myriad existing data sets, identifies the value and challenges of the potential architecture, and specifies institutional strategies to develop and maintain the architecture. The report is especially valuable for (1) its analysis of the strengths and weaknesses of a wide range of data sources; (2) the development of a national freight data architecture definition that is scalable at the national, state, regional, and local levels; and (3) a better understanding of the challenges that might block the implementation of a national freight data architecture as well as candidate strategies for developing, adopting, and maintaining the data architecture. This report lays the foundation for the development of such a data architecture.

Public and private decisionmakers must understand the freight transportation system, its use, its role in economic development, its environmental impact, as well as other consequences in order to respond effectively to growing logistical requirements for businesses and households. This understanding draws on many disparate data sources covering commodity movements, relationships among sectors of the economy, international trade, freight traffic, supply chains, and transportation services and infrastructure. These data sources are difficult to link into useful information because they are collected under various definitions and time scales, geographic levels, and aspects of transportation. Efforts to bridge these differences with analytical techniques or new data collections tend to be ad hoc or cover only part of the freight transportation universe. Several studies and conferences by TRB have called for a national freight data architecture to link existing data sets and guide new data collections. However, none of these calls defined what is meant by data architecture or how it would be designed and implemented.

Under NCFRP Project 12, the Texas Transportation Institute was asked to (1) review systems, databases, and architectures that might be used as a potential reference for the development of a national freight data architecture; (2) develop a formal definition for a national freight data architecture; (3) identify high-level categories of data architecture components; (4) identify potential implementation approaches; (5) develop a list of specifications for the freight data architecture; and (6) identify challenges and strategies related to the implementation of a national freight data architecture.

CONTENTS

Note: Many of the photographs, figures, and tables in this report have been converted from color to grayscale for printing. The electronic version of the report (posted on the Web at www.trb.org) retains the color versions.

SUMMARY

Guidance for Developing a Freight Transportation Data Architecture

Introduction

The movement of freight in the United States continues to grow, causing congestion along corridors and at network nodes such as seaports, land ports of entry, truck and rail terminals, and airports. It is critical to have accurate, comprehensive, and timely information about freight movements and the impact of these movements on the transportation network in order to make sound investment decisions to improve and optimize the freight transportation system.

This report documents the results of a study to develop specifications for content and structure of a national freight data architecture that serves the needs of public and private decisionmakers at the national, state, regional, and local levels. It is worth noting that the purpose of NCFRP Project 12 was to develop requirements and specifications for a national freight data architecture, not to develop the data architecture (which would be a logical next step after identifying those requirements and specifications). The research team undertook the following activities to address these research needs:

- Completed a review of systems, databases, and architectures that might be used as a potential reference for the development of a national freight data architecture;
- Conducted surveys and follow-up interviews, interviews with subject matter experts, and a peer exchange with freight transportation stakeholders;
- Developed a formal definition for a national freight data architecture;
- Identified high-level categories of data architecture components;
- Identified potential implementation approaches;
- Developed a list of specifications for a national freight data architecture; and
- Identified challenges and strategies related to the implementation of a national freight data architecture.

Data Sources, Systems, and Architectures

Various listings, links, and summaries of systems, databases, architectures, and other related documents that pertain to freight transportation data are available in the literature. Although there is a wealth of sources of information that pertain to freight transportation, a comprehensive catalog of freight-related data sources at different geographic levels (including national, state, regional, and local levels) does not exist. As a reference, the research team conducted a review of a sample of freight-related data sources at the national level to complement or otherwise extend existing listings. This sample is obviously not comprehensive. For example, it does not reference datasets that state, regional, and local entities need to collect to supplement or augment national-level datasets. Although the sample of data sources evaluated does not include all the potential data sources that deal with freight transportation, it is useful because it provides a sample of the typical national-level data sources that would need to be included in a national freight data architecture. A few systems and architectures were of particular interest because of the lessons that could be derived from the processes that led to their development. The analysis included topics such as purpose, content, institutional arrangements used for developing and maintaining the system or architecture; challenges and issues faced in creating and maintaining the architecture or system; strategies and methods for dealing with data integration issues; and adaptability to serve evolving purposes and data sources.

Online Surveys, Interviews, and Peer Exchange

The research team conducted a planner and analyst survey, a shipper survey, and a motor carrier survey (as well as follow-up interviews) to gather information about freight data uses and needs. The research team also conducted interviews with subject matter experts to address specific items of interest to the research. The purpose of the planner and analyst survey was to gather information from government planners, analysts, and other similar freight-related stakeholders. Respondents were involved in all modes of transportation, including air, rail, truck, pipelines, and water. Respondents indicated that they use freight data to support the production of a wide range of public-sector transportation planning documents, adding weight to the notion that the national freight data architecture should support a variety of freight-related processes. Respondents reported using and/or needing data at various levels of geographic coverage and resolution. The feedback on unmet data needs complement similar findings in the literature.

The purpose of the shipper survey was to gather general information from the shipper community regarding freight data uses and needs, as well as willingness to share data with other freight-related stakeholders. Feedback from respondents indicates that the shipper industry collects large amounts of data. Many shippers and logistics service providers transmit data electronically using electronic data interchange (EDI) technologies. However, accessing data from shippers and logistics service providers for transportation planning applications, beyond aggregated data from commercial data providers and national survey campaigns such as the Commodity Flow Survey (CFS), is not necessarily straightforward. For example, while a data record might characterize a commodity as well as origin and destination locations, the route data component may be missing unless the carrier movement data are included. In addition, the shipper stakeholders interviewed indicated they could not comment on their companies' ability or willingness to share data for freight transportation planning purposes (particularly on a load-by-load basis, given its proprietary and confidential nature). Subsequent feedback obtained at the peer exchange (see below) highlighted a number of strategies to address this issue, including initiating discussions about data sharing at a sufficiently high administrative level—since low-ranking personnel might know the data, but frequently do not have the authority or permission to discuss data sharing options. Involving trade associations rather than individual firms might also be beneficial.

The purpose of the motor carrier survey was to gather information from the motor carrier community about freight data uses and needs, as well as willingness to share data with external freight-related stakeholders. Carriers handle large amounts of disaggregated data during the course of their business operations. Increasingly, carriers use EDI standards and applications. However, the amount of shipment information detail varies according to the type of carrier. For example, truckload (TL) carriers, who tend to bill customers on a per-mile basis or by using a flat rate, rarely collect detailed commodity data. In addition, TL carriers are less likely to collect data on tonnage hauled or tare-level data. By comparison, less-than-truckload (LTL) carriers typically bill customers using a rate structure based on shipment weight, origin, destination, and freight classification. However, LTL carriers tend to favor a freight-all-kinds rating structure that assigns a general freight classification to all shipments regardless of freight commodity or type. As opposed to TL carriers, LTL carriers are more likely to track total tonnage. Motor carrier reservations about sharing proprietary and confidential data were related to the need to develop mechanisms to protect proprietary and confidential information and to maintain the anonymity of carriers and customers. In general, carriers would need to know in advance the specific uses of the data and, in return, would expect information in the form of industry benchmarking metrics. It is worth noting that developing metrics of interest to the private sector is part of the scope of work of NCFRP Project 3 "Performance Measures for Freight Transportation."

In conjunction with the 2009 North American Freight Flows Conference held in Irvine, CA, the research team organized a peer exchange to discuss preliminary research findings; request feedback; and facilitate a dialogue on implementation strategies to develop, adopt, and maintain a national freight data architecture. Participants included representatives of federal, state, regional, university, and private-sector agencies. To encourage participation and discussion, attendees received background materials such as relevant research topic summaries and breakout group agendas and discussion objectives. Feedback from peer exchange participants included recommendations for changes to initial research findings as well as a list of issues, challenges, and strategies to consider during the implementation of the national freight data architecture.

National Freight Data Architecture Definition

Taking into consideration the results of the literature review, as well as feedback from surveys, follow-up interviews, and the peer exchange, the research team developed the following generic definition for a national freight data architecture:

> The national freight data architecture is the manner in which data elements are organized and integrated for freight transportation-related applications or business processes. The data architecture includes the necessary set of tools that describe related functions or roles, components where those roles reside or apply, and data flows that connect roles and components at different domain and aggregation levels.

Depending on the specific level of implementation chosen for the data architecture, this generic definition could be fine-tuned as follows:

- **Single-application approach.** In this case, the national freight data architecture would become the manner in which data elements are organized and integrated for *a specific* freight application or business process at the national level (e.g., commodity flows).
- **Intermediate approaches (depending on the number of applications).** In this case, the national freight data architecture would become the manner in which data elements are organized and integrated for *a specific set* of applications at the national, state, regional, and local levels. A large number of intermediate approaches is possible, depending on the business processes and geographic levels involved. For example, an intermediate implementation approach could include commodity flows at the national, state, and regional levels. Another, more encompassing, intermediate implementation approach could include commodity flows, safety, and pavement impacts at the national, state, regional, and local levels.
- **Holistic, all-encompassing approach.** In this case, the national freight data architecture would become the manner in which data elements are organized and integrated for *all* freight transportation-related applications or business processes at the national, state, regional, and local levels.

For any of these implementation options, the data architecture would include the necessary set of tools that describe related functions or roles, components where those roles reside or apply, and data flows that connect roles and components.

National Freight Data Architecture Value

From the documentation and information gathered during the research, the research team identified the following list of benefits that, together, provide a statement of value for the national freight data architecture:

- Better understanding of the different business processes that affect freight transportation at different levels of coverage and resolution;
- Better understanding of the supply chain, which should help transportation planners to identify strategies for improving freight transportation infrastructure;
- Better understanding of the role that different public-sector and private-sector stakeholders play on freight transportation;
- Better understanding of the need for standards to assist in data exchange;
- Systematic, coordinated development of reference datasets (e.g., comprehensive commodity code crosswalk tables);
- Systematic inventory of freight transportation data sources;
- Systematic inventory of user and data needs that are prerequisites for the development of freight data management systems;
- Use as a reference for the identification of locations where there may be freight data redundancy and inefficiencies;
- Use as a reference for requesting funding allocations in the public and private sectors; and
- Use as a reference for the development of outreach, professional development, and training materials.

In practice, the value of the national freight data architecture is also a function of the costs associated with its implementation. Quantifiable data about expected benefits and costs are currently not available (benefit-cost analyses need to occur both at the beginning and at different phases of implementation of the national freight data architecture). However, it is clear from the documentation and information gathered during the research that the "do-nothing" alternative (i.e., not implementing the national freight data architecture) is costly, ineffective, and unsustainable. Therefore, the research team's recommendation is to pursue the national freight data architecture following a scalable implementation path in which the national freight data architecture starts with one application at one or two levels of decisionmaking and then adds applications and levels of decisionmaking as needed or according to a predetermined implementation plan until, eventually, reaching the maximum net value.

National Freight Data Architecture Components

The research team identified the following categories of components to include in the national freight data architecture:

- Physical transportation components,
- Cargo or freight,
- Freight functions or roles,
- Business processes,
- Data sources,

- Freight-related data,
- Freight data models,
- Freight data standards, and
- User interface and supporting documentation.

Figure 1 shows a high-level modular conceptualization and lists different categories of components. The diagram recognizes the scalable nature of the national freight data architecture and enables the production of various diagram versions (as well as tabular representations) depending on what implementation level to pursue. For example, for a single-application data architecture that only focuses on commodity flows at the national level, it may not be necessary to depict (at least not in detail) other freight functions and business processes. Similarly, not all data standards would need to be considered, and the requirements for user interfaces to support that data architecture would be relatively minor. The diagram in Figure 1 is only one example of potentially many different types of diagrams that can be used to depict interactions among freight transportation components.

National Freight Data Architecture Recommendations and Specifications

In addition to the list of categories and components, the research team put together a list of recommendations for the development and implementation of the national freight data architecture. For convenience, the recommendations are written in the form of specifications to guide and monitor the implementation of the data architecture as follows:

- Adopt a definition for the national freight data architecture that is generic, scalable, and understood and accepted by the freight transportation community (see proposed definition above);
- Compare candidate data architecture concepts;
- Develop implementation plan for national freight data architecture components;
- Develop lists of components to include in the national freight data architecture;
- Develop and implement protocols for continuous stakeholder participation;
- Conduct data gap analysis;
- Conduct data disaggregation need analysis;
- Assume a distributed approach (as opposed to a centralized approach) to freight data repository implementations;
- Use a systems engineering approach for developing the national freight data architecture;
- Use standard information technology tools and procedures;
- Develop and/or use standardized terminology and definitions for each data architecture component developed;
- Implement strong privacy protection strategies; and
- Establish integration points with other data architectures and standards.

Readers should note that the list of specifications is preliminary and might need refinement during the process of building the data architecture.

Challenges and Strategies

The research team identified relevant issues and challenges that might block the implementation of the national freight data architecture as well as candidate strategies for developing, adopting, and maintaining the data architecture. The challenges were in the following categories: technical, policy, economic/financial, and stakeholder buy-in and consensus.

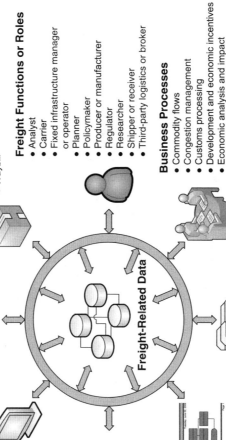

User Interface and Supporting Documentation
- Web-based information clearinghouse
- Outreach and training materials

Freight Data Standards
- Commodity and product classification standards
  - CPC
  - HMIS
  - HS
  - NAPCS
  - NMFC
  - NST 2007
  - PLU
  - SCTG
  - STCC
- Industrial classification standards
  - ISIC
  - NAICS
  - SIC
  - SITC
- Data exchange standards
  - ANSI ASC X12 standards
  - UN/EDIFACT standards
  - OASIS UBL standards
  - FIPS PUB 161-2
  - National ITS standards
  - FGDC-sponsored standards (including metadata)
  - Other standards
  - ITDS SDS
  - METS
  - Vehicle classification standards

Physical Transportation Components
- Vehicle
- Container
- Transportation network
- Traffic control system

Cargo or Freight
- Bill of lading
- Commodity
- Invoice
- Item or product
- Purchase order
- Shipment
- Waybill

Freight Data Models
- Business process model
- Conceptual model
- Logical model
- Physical model
- Data dictionary
- Metadata

Data Sources
- Administrative records
- Census
- Data standards
- Mandatory reporting required by laws and regulations
- Surveys
- Other private-sector data
- Other public-sector data

Freight Functions or Roles
- Analyst
- Carrier
- Fixed infrastructure manager or operator
- Planner
- Policymaker
- Producer or manufacturer
- Regulator
- Researcher
- Shipper or receiver
- Third-party logistics or broker

Business Processes
- Commodity flows
- Congestion management
- Customs processing
- Development and economic incentives
- Economic analysis and impact
- Energy and climate change
- Environmental impacts
- Hazardous material handling
- Incident response
- Industry and state needs
- International trade
- Logistics management
- Marketing and grant funding
- On-board security monitoring
- Planning and forecasting
- Policy development
- Roadside safety inspection
- Routing and dispatching
- Safety analysis
- Transportation infrastructure analysis, design, and construction
- Transportation operations
- Workforce development and training

Freight-Related Data
- Descriptions of products shipped or received
- Shipment origins and destinations
- Shipment weight
- Freight volumes
- Manifests and waybills
- Carrier used
- Railroad tonnage data
- Commodity inventories
- Licensed carrier data
- Vehicle inventories
- Business directories
- Employment by freight activity
- Import and export statistics
- Mine output data
- Economic data
- Transportation infrastructure inventory and condition
- Pipeline volumes
- Traffic volumes
- Distribution warehouse truck traffic data
- Travel time, speed, and delay data
- Traffic bottlenecks
- Oversize and overweight permitting and routing data
- Safety data
- Fuel statistics
- Emissions data and estimates

Notes:
1) Categories and components are provided for illustration purposes, are not exhaustive, and may be subject to change.
2) Not all categories and components apply to all freight-related business processes.

Figure 1. National freight data architecture framework and components.

- **Technical challenges.** Technical challenges refer to issues (e.g., technological limitations, hardware and software incompatibilities, and standards incompatibilities) that might impede the successful implementation of the data architecture. Examples include the following:
  - Feasibility of different implementation approaches;
  - Data storage requirements;
  - Feasibility of updated data entry protocols to eliminate data redundancies and support standardized data entry procedures;
  - Conversion of commodity code classifications;
  - Data life cycle and usefulness to support the decisionmaking process by public and private stakeholders;
  - Variability in data quality control practices, which affects data accuracy, completeness, and timeliness;
  - Differences in terminology, data item definitions, and data implementations among freight data stakeholders;
  - Prioritization of data architecture components;
  - Integration between shipper and carrier data to characterize commodity movements properly; and
  - Data confidentiality and security concerns.
- **Policy challenges.** The national freight data architecture might fail if required policies, both in the public and private sectors, fail or are not feasible. Examples of policy challenges include the following:
  - Homeland security concerns, which might limit the dissemination of certain freight-related data;
  - Impact on current private-sector data collection initiatives; and
  - Competitive and proprietary (privacy) concerns with the concept of public-sector agencies having access to private-sector data.
- **Economic and financial challenges.** The national freight data architecture might fail if the perceived costs associated with its implementation exceed the benefits that stakeholders would receive. Examples of economic and financial challenges include the following:
  - Cost of data collection, storage, and quality assurance;
  - Benefits and costs related to data disaggregation requirements for different business processes;
  - Data life cycle and usefulness to support the decisionmaking process by public and private stakeholders;
  - Cost to acquire private-sector data; and
  - Cost to implement robust data confidentiality and data security measures.
- **Stakeholder buy-in and consensus.** The national freight data architecture might fail if there is no stakeholder buy-in or consensus about the potential benefits that could result from implementing the data architecture. Examples of related issues include the following:
  - Reluctance of stakeholders to participate if there is no clarity regarding justification and anticipated benefits;
  - Confidentiality clauses in supply chain contracts, which might impede data sharing for transportation planning purposes;
  - Perception that data collected as part of a national freight data collection program could validate projects of national significance at the expense of small or rural communities;
  - Ability of carriers to provide data about loads they move;
  - Risk of low stakeholder participation, which could decrease data reliability; and
  - Adequacy of data standards.

Strategies to ensure a successful implementation of the national freight data architecture include the following:

- Implementation levels
  - Develop and compare candidate data architecture concepts,
  - Identify business process and implementation level priorities,
  - Develop high-quality data architecture concepts and applications that address the needs of the highest priority items first, and
  - Identify data needs at the finest disaggregation level and implement data collection and data storage plans at that level.
- Relationships with leaders, champions, and stakeholders
  - Identify data architecture leaders and champions;
  - Engage the national freight data architecture champions early;
  - Maintain good communication channels with the various stakeholders during all phases of the development and implementation of the national freight transportation data architecture;
  - Identify funding mechanisms for the implementation of the data architecture;
  - Develop brochures, presentations, and other materials that explain the national freight data architecture, its scope, high-level components, and what it expects to accomplish;
  - Deliver effective messages on how the national freight data architecture will assist stakeholders in the identification of strategies to address a variety of freight-related issues ranging from data collection to analysis and reporting;
  - Deliver messages that provide clear, concise answers to the various challenges highlighted in the previous section;
  - Articulate benefits of participation by the private sector; and
  - Identify opportunities for partnerships with the private sector (e.g., through public-private partnerships) to make data accessible for transportation planning purposes in a cost-effective manner.
- Performance measures and effectiveness
  - Develop criteria for measuring effectiveness in the implementation of the national freight data architecture,
  - Identify major progress milestones,
  - Tie the implementation of the national freight data architecture to the development of metrics or performance measures that could benefit the entire freight transportation community, and
  - Accelerate the implementation of programs such as EFM and the freight performance measurement program.
- Lessons learned from the implementation and maintenance of existing freight-related systems and architectures
  - Develop systems that are relevant to stakeholders, include adequate stakeholder participation, and provide incentives to encourage participation—particularly in the case of state and local entities;
  - Clearly define expected outcomes and development and coordination plan;
  - Articulate programs well; provide clear, uniform guidance; and provide good documentation;
  - Develop applications that rely on widely used data standards;
  - Develop and compare candidate architecture concepts;
  - Consider federal legislation to support and develop the program;
  - Develop tools to measure benefits and costs early;

- Integrate archived data needs into frameworks and architectures early and develop data programs that use industry standards;
- Implement interagency data exchange programs with centralized data coordination;
- Use available data sources and develop long-term plans while keeping systems flexible to respond to changes and new data sources;
- Schedule major and regular revisions effectively while avoiding scope creep;
- Develop systems that are consistent with input data limitations;
- Develop applications with backward compatibility;
- Evaluate data disaggregation level requirements to ensure statistical significance;
- Provide adequate resources for data collection, fully understand the implications of small sample sizes, and continue to involve the U.S. Census Bureau for the use of survey instruments;
- Emphasize data access, quality, reliability, confidentiality, and integrity;
- Participate in the standards development process;
- Create crosswalks to ensure compatibility of survey data internally over time and externally across other datasets;
- Involve stakeholders early and often through various mechanisms and technologies; and
- Develop and implement professional capacity and training programs early.

One of the strategies for implementation mentioned is to develop and compare candidate data architecture concepts. Peer exchange participants highlighted that implementing a comprehensive data architecture at once with no testing of options prior to making a decision about the correct approach would be too risky. Participants also favored the concept of developing and comparing several alternative approaches.

A recommendation from peer exchange participants was to use NCFRP as an avenue for funding the development of alternative data architecture concepts. Participants indicated that the request for proposals should outline clear objectives while leaving the definition of approaches to the research team(s) selected. An idea discussed was to develop the data architecture around scenarios or themes, such as business areas or processes, levels of government, or economic activity. Activities in connection with each scenario or theme would include structuring a competition for research teams (each of which would include a university partner, a private-sector partner, and a government-level partner) to develop and test competing data architecture concepts, making sure to include multimodal components in the scenarios and tests, and conduct a follow-up evaluation.

CHAPTER 1

Introduction

Background

In 2006, the nation's transportation system moved more than 20 billion tons of goods valued at close to $15 trillion (*1*). The movement of freight in the country has more than doubled in the last 15 years, and it is expected to continue growing at a similar pace, with a projected level of 37 billion tons in 2035. This growth challenges the national transportation infrastructure, resulting in congestion along corridors and at the nodes of the network, including seaports, land ports of entry, truck and rail terminals, and airports.

It is important to have accurate, comprehensive, and timely information in order to make sound investment decisions to improve and optimize the freight transportation system (*2*). A large number of stakeholders need access to freight transportation data. For example, federal, state, and local level transportation planning agencies require freight transportation information to identify operations and infrastructure improvements to the transportation system. Likewise, the private sector requires accurate, timely information on freight movements as well as accurate, timely information about the characteristics and operating conditions of the transportation network. Frequently, the need for data is on a real-time, or near-real-time, basis. High-quality data enable private-sector stakeholders to make informed investment decisions as well as informed operational decisions.

Examples of real-world situations where the need for an integrated approach to freight data is critical include the following:

- **Commodity classification codes.** A western state department of transportation (DOT) is currently developing a forecast of commodity flows by mode. Efforts by the state DOT to merge data from different studies had to address commodity code compatibility issues because state data used Standard Transportation Commodity Code (STCC) classifications, while regional forecasts used Standard Classification of Transported Goods (SCTG) codes. This issue was resolved, but only after a laborious, expensive process. A unified commodity classification system would have avoided that problem. Around the country, states and metropolitan planning organizations (MPOs) that develop freight forecasting tools collect data from various sources, but the commodity classification codes contained within those sources are not always compatible, making analyses of commodity data difficult and time consuming.

- **Freight data and performance measure definitions.** As part of FHWA's Freight Performance Measurement (FPM) initiative, there was an interest in collecting border crossing travel time and delay data. Before collecting any data, it was necessary to agree on what border crossing "travel time" meant since different stakeholders might use different definitions and data collection procedures. For example, one stakeholder would only measure the time for a freight shipment to go through the border crossing process on one side of the border. However, other stakeholders would consider the total time to go through both sides of the border. Obviously, defining border crossing delay was only possible after agreeing to a common definition for border crossing travel time. Measuring delay also required the definition of a common reference against which travel times would be measured. The lack of standard definitions often leads to data incompatibilities and duplication of data collection efforts.

- **Federal, state, and local freight data collection efforts.** A large Midwest MPO covers a metropolitan area that comprises 6 counties and over 10 million people. The area includes several Class I railroads, 2 passenger transit systems, over 20 multimodal terminals, toll roads, and the confluences of several "smart" corridors. Many freight nodes generate traffic that moves within county boundaries. These movements do not appear on purchased transportation databases. Collecting origin-destination (O-D) data is expensive and time consuming. Many state and local agencies are interested in O-D freight data, but do not have enough resources to collect this type of data. As a result, those agencies use O-D data collected at the national level, even though the national data do not provide a clear picture of O-D data at a county or city level. In some cases, state and local agencies end up developing customized tools to address their needs, frequently at great expense. However, not all state or local agencies have this capability. Access to finer resolution O-D data collected at the national level would provide state and local transportation planners with a valuable long-term analysis tool for making freight-related infrastructure improvements.

- **Regional freight data integration.** In a large metropolitan area where three state boundaries are within a 60-mi radius, there are multiple sources of freight data, including data collected by the states, data collected by the MPO, and data purchased from a large commercial data provider. Reconciling or validating these separate databases is difficult due to the variability in time periods, data collection protocols, and potential overlaps, which, in turn, makes it difficult to build a common database with elements from each source.

- **Data to support public–private partnerships.** In a rural part of the nation where the Class I rail carriers have "rationalized" service and facilities, there is an interest in public–private partnership projects. These projects must have public support to attract private investment because the primary benefit is social and business development. In order to complete benefit-cost information to help attract private investment for these rural projects, it is necessary to obtain data to properly characterize rail traffic in the region. Unfortunately, it is virtually impossible for the analysts to obtain this information.

- **Regional freight data understanding and integration.** A paper manufacturer purchases logs from landowners in a tri-state area. The logs and resulting paper products are essentially commodities that compete primarily on price. Companies in the area would benefit from a pooled transportation program and an optimization approach with a multimodal solution (truck and rail) that addresses multistate rules. In order to exchange transportation pricing data (which otherwise would not be allowed), it is necessary to form a cooperative or a shipper association. However, the three states involved have different truck size and weight restrictions, do not have data forms for similar periods, and cannot link O-D pair trips across state boundaries. The railroad, due to recent mergers, wholesaling efforts, and a centralized sales approach, does not have a good understanding of local conditions and is closing rail access points due to the region's "poor performance."

- **Oversize/overweight permitting.** A southern state that processes a large number of oversize/overweight permits is frequently tasked with permit requests for oversize or over-

weight loads that must be unloaded at a seaport and then transported over state (and sometimes county) roads to another state. Routing is difficult because of the lack of relevant integrated information at both ends of the routing process, including information about acceptable routes in neighboring states. In one recent example, a load coming from Asia had to be transferred to another port first because land routes connecting to the first port where the load arrived were not adequate.

- **Short-haul trip optimization.** In a port town where it is necessary to move international and domestic containers (using a combination of loads and empties, bare chassis, and bob tail trucks) between rail, port terminals, container yards, customers, and trucking terminals, data to help address empty miles and truck trip reduction needs are not available. Due to the intense competition for this short-haul business, primarily within a trucking/brokerage business model, efforts to create a shared data clearinghouse have not achieved desired results.

- **Freight transportation performance measures.** Traffic congestion negatively affects freight mobility, causes huge losses to the private sector, and results in undesirable environmental impacts. However, there is no adequate database of performance measures nationwide that analysts could use to quantify those impacts accurately. The identification of those measures, and the underlying data that will be needed for their assessment, is a critical requirement for the identification of sound freight transportation strategies around the country.

- **Truck routing.** In a southern state, motor carriers have two options to travel through a very congested growing metropolitan area—they can either use the existing non-tolled Interstate highway (shorter distance) or use a new tolled facility that bypasses the metropolitan area (longer distance). Traffic conditions on the non-tolled facility can rapidly change from acceptable to stop-and-go. Because of intense competition and low profit margins, some carriers would like to be able to make routing decisions based on accurate current, as well as anticipated, traffic conditions. However, this information is not available.

- **Decisionmaking process in the private sector.** The dynamics of domestic and international trade, influenced by the rapid growth of e-commerce, require an increasing number of shipments in smaller quantities. Both shippers and carriers require information to optimize distribution networks and supply chains, making it critical to have access to accurate, timely information on freight movements as well as accurate, timely information about the characteristics and operating conditions of the transportation network. Frequent updates on the operational status of the transportation system would allow the private sector to make routing decisions dynamically, thereby reducing delays, costs, and emissions. Access to up-to-date benchmarking metrics and statistics would also facilitate the decisionmaking process in the private sector. However, freight transportation data and indicators are frequently dated.

- **Truck trip generation rates.** Truck trip generation is an essential metric in a public planner's tool kit. Existing data include warehouse locations and traffic volumes on the links that connect these facilities to other supply chain locations. However, other pieces of information are missing (e.g., whether a warehouse facility is a live load/unload business, provides for drop and hook trucking operations, or is supported by truck load [TL] or less-than-truckload [LTL] service). Likewise, although it is possible to measure or estimate the square feet of warehouse space, there is no information about its cubic capacity. However, the number of trucks generated from a facility can vary greatly depending on the ceiling height.

To respond effectively to current and anticipated freight data requirements, public and private decisionmakers must understand the freight transportation system, its use, and its role in economic development. As Figure 2 suggests, one way to understand freight transportation is by analyzing commodity movements, trade, and relationships among different sec- tors of the economy. In reality, as the real-world examples above demonstrate, understanding freight transportation requires taking into consideration many other aspects, a small sample of which includes operating conditions of the transportation network, traffic congestion, environmental impacts, and safety.

Although there are many ongoing freight data collection efforts, these efforts are frequently inadequate in terms of scope, coverage, geographic and/or temporal resolution, quality, and access to data. Efforts to bridge these gaps with analytical techniques and/or additional data collection programs tend to be ad hoc and cover only limited aspects of the entire freight transportation data spectrum.

The transportation community has recognized the urgent need to address this problem. For example, the TRB's 2003 *Special Report 276: A Concept for a National Freight Data Program,* recommended a framework for developing national commodity movement data, with a goal to facilitate data fusion and fill data gaps in order to develop a comprehensive picture of freight flows (4). This report evolved from a 2001 conference in Saratoga Springs, NY, which concluded that currently available data were inadequate to support the requirements of analysts and policymakers and recommended a framework for the development of national freight data (5).

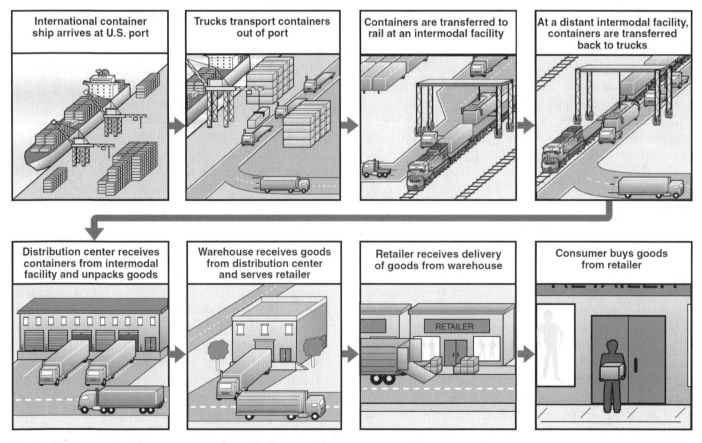

Figure 2. Example of movement of goods from port to consumer (3).

The proposed framework in *Special Report 276* included an advisory committee to oversee the detailed design of a multi-faceted survey program, a comprehensive survey and data gathering program, a national freight database, a freight data synthesis program to fill data gaps, and supplemental data collection activities (Figure 3).

Special Report 276 recognized the availability of data sources such as the Commodity Flow Survey (CFS), the Vehicle Inventory and Use Survey (VIUS) (now discontinued), the Carload Waybill Sample, and the Waterborne Commerce of the United States (WCUS) database. The report recognized the potential for data availability resulting from the implementation of initiatives such as the Freight Analysis Framework (FAF) and the Automated Commercial Environment/International Trade Data System (ACE/ITDS). The report also recognized the increasing importance of alternative data collection methods (e.g., through EDI programs and intelligent transportation system [ITS] implementations), and recommended the implementation of strategies to encourage data collection and synthesis by public- and private-sector organizations. Noting the unique position of the federal government to provide the necessary leadership to ensure a successful implementation of a framework for national commodity movement data, the report recommended that the Bureau of Transportation Statistics (BTS) assume that

leadership role. In general, the report highlighted the need to conduct an assessment of the strengths and weaknesses of a wide range of data sources as a prerequisite for the development of the national framework.

Special Report 276 described the proposed framework for national commodity movement data at a high conceptual level. As a result, it would be inappropriate to treat the report as a prescription for detailed framework data components or requirements. For example, the report recommended capturing the following data items to describe important commodity movement characteristics: origin and destination; commodity characteristics, weight, and value; modes of shipment; routing and time of day; and vehicle/vessel type and configuration. However, it only briefly addressed other critical related issues such as privacy and data confidentiality issues, data fusion challenges, agency roles, and security considerations.

In 2009, NCHRP Project 8-36, Task 79, proposed a high-level framework for a prototype web-based freight data exchange network (Figure 4) (6). In the framework, the data exchange network (Figure 4) would be a centralized data repository where data providers and users enter and/or access commodity movement-related datasets, metadata, data quality reports, and reference materials. The web-based data exchange network would enable users to extract, transform,

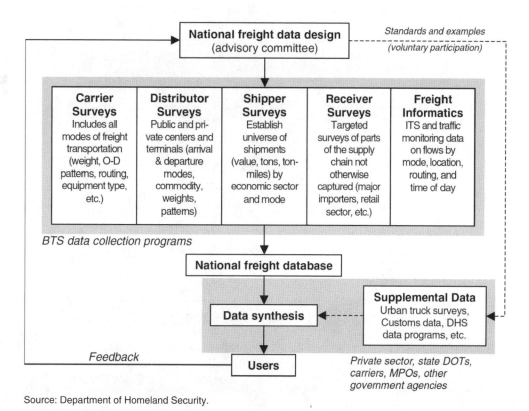

Source: Department of Homeland Security.

Figure 3. **TRB's Special Report 276: Proposed Framework for a National Freight Data Program (4).**

14

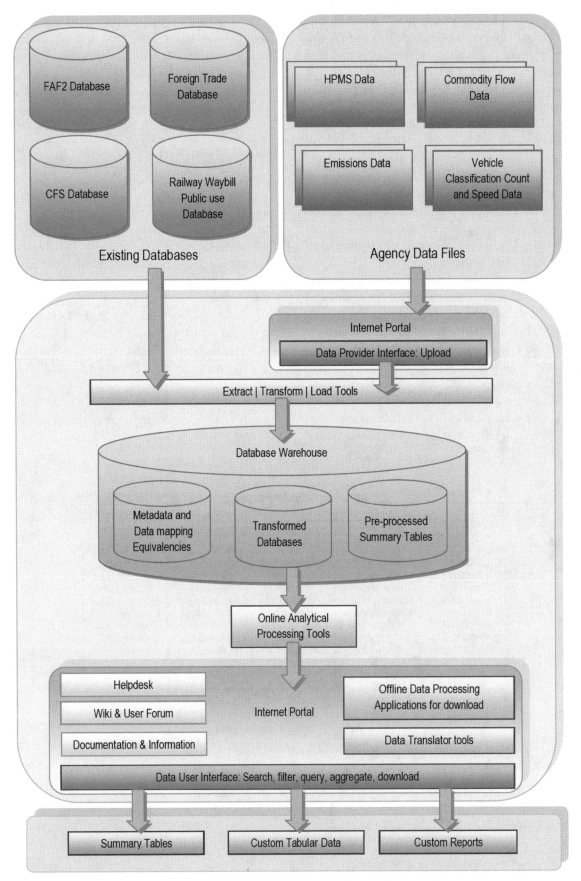

Figure 4. NCHRP Project 8-36—Task 79's proposed freight data exchange network framework (6).

and query datasets. The data warehouse would include meta-data for the transformed datasets and pre-processed summary tables. As in the case of the framework proposed in TRB's *Special Report 276,* the focus of the NCHRP Project 8-36 Task 79 freight data exchange network was commodity movement data.

As part of the Upper Midwest Freight Corridor Study, which covered several upper Midwest states as well the provinces of Ontario and Manitoba in Canada, researchers developed a system called Midwest FreightView that enables users to connect remotely to freight datasets located at the University of Toledo (7). The system includes a viewer that depicts features such as highways, rail lines, ports, and inter-modal terminals. The system contains datasets from agencies at the federal, state (or provincial), and regional levels. In addition, the database contains regional economic data, including employment figures, number and locations of establishments, and types of commodities produced within each portion of the region.

The need for reliable freight transportation data also has been identified in the U.S. DOT's proposed Framework for a National Freight Policy, which includes the following objectives (8):

- Objective 1: Improve the operations of the existing freight transportation system.
- Objective 2: Add physical capacity to the freight transportation system in places where investment makes economic sense.
- Objective 3: Better align all costs and benefits among parties affected by the freight system to improve productivity.
- Objective 4: Reduce or remove statutory, regulatory, and institutional barriers to improved freight transportation performance.
- Objective 5: Proactively identify and address emerging transportation needs.
- Objective 6: Maximize the safety and security of the freight transportation system.
- Objective 7: Mitigate and better manage the environmental, health, energy, and community impacts of freight transportation.

Each objective, strategy, and tactic in the freight policy framework requires collecting, maintaining, and using reliable data. Recognizing this need, the framework includes the following strategies to address freight data needs:

- Strategy 4.4: Actively engage and support the establishment of international standards to facilitate freight movement.
- Strategy 5.1: Develop data and analytical capacity for making future investment decisions.

Clearly, the range of data needs to support the national freight policy framework is quite wide and covers a variety of freight-related business processes, including trade and supply chain; planning, design, construction, operations, and maintenance of freight transportation networks; environmental and energy impacts; safety; and security.

Research Objectives

The overarching theme behind NCFRP Project 12 was the need for accurate, comprehensive, timely freight transportation data at different levels, as well as the need for a holistic approach to freight transportation data. More specifically, NCFRP 12 was set up to identify specifications for a national freight data architecture that would facilitate freight-related statistical and economic analyses; support the decisionmaking process by public and private stakeholders at the national, state, regional, and local levels; and enable the acquisition and maintenance of critical data needed to identify freight-related transportation needs. Specific NCFRP Project 12 objectives included the following:

- Develop specifications for content and structure of a national freight data architecture that serves the needs of public and private decisionmakers at the national, state, regional, and local levels;
- Identify the value and challenges of the potential data architecture; and
- Specify institutional strategies to develop and maintain the data architecture.

In providing a frame of reference for the rest of this report, it is worth noting that the scope of NCFRP Project 12 was to develop requirements and specifications for a national freight data architecture, not to develop the data architecture (which would be a logical next step after identifying those requirements and specifications). In addition, although Chapter 4 includes a formal definition and scope for a national freight data architecture, it may be useful at this point to clarify what is, and what is not, a data architecture. In general, a data architecture can be defined as the manner and process used to organize and integrate data components. This definition is similar to others found in the literature. It follows that a data architecture is *not* a database (databases may be built based on data architectures); a data model, a data standard, a specification, or a framework (these elements could be components of a data architecture); a system architecture (a system architecture could use data architecture components); a simulation or optimization model; or an institutional program.

The remainder of this report summarizes the research findings as follows:

- Chapter 2 includes a discussion of systems, databases, and architectures that might be used as a potential reference for the development of a national freight data architecture;
- Chapter 3 includes a summary of data needs and the results of online questionnaires and subsequent interviews with freight stakeholders;
- Chapter 4 provides an outline and draft requirements for a national freight data architecture, as well as challenges and strategies related to the implementation of a national freight data architecture; and
- Chapter 5 includes relevant conclusions and recommendations.
- Appendix A of the contractor's final report, available on the project webpage, provides freight transportation data sources.

CHAPTER 2

Data Sources, Systems, and Architectures

Introduction

This chapter includes a discussion of systems, databases, and architectures that might be used as a potential reference for the development of a national freight data architecture. As previously described, the purpose of NCFRP Project 12 was to develop specifications for a national freight data architecture that could support the decisionmaking process by both public *and* private stakeholders not just at the national level, but also at the state, regional, and local levels. As the real-world examples in Chapter 1 showed, supporting such a wide spectrum of decisionmaking needs requires using a wide range of data sources. The literature review in this chapter includes a general description of available data sources as well as a detailed discussion of several systems and architectures that were of particular interest because of the processes that led to their development, which could be used as lessons learned while developing a national freight data architecture.

Data Sources

A variety of listings, links, and summaries of systems, databases, architectures, and other related documents that pertain to freight transportation data are available in the literature. A small sample of documents that contain freight transportation data-related listings includes the following:

- FHWA listings of freight data sources (*9, 10*);
- FHWA report: *Quick Response Freight Manual II* (*11*);
- BTS report: *Directory of Transportation Data Sources* (*12*);
- BTS report: *A Preliminary Roadmap for the American Freight Data Program* (*13*); and
- Texas Department of Transportation report: *State-of-the-Practice in Freight Data: A Review of Available Freight Data in the U.S.* (*14*).

Although there is a wealth of sources of information that pertain to freight transportation, a comprehensive catalog of freight-related data sources at different geographic levels (including national, state, regional, and local levels) does not exist. As a reference, the research team conducted a review of a sample of freight-related data sources at the national level to complement or otherwise extend existing listings. Table 1 provides the following information:

- **Freight data source/dataset.** This column provides a listing of freight transportation data sources reviewed in this report. In total, the research team reviewed 49 freight data sources. For convenience, Table 1 groups data sources according to the following categories: public-sector data sources; private-sector data sources; freight-related architectures, frameworks, programs, and standards; and initiatives under development.
- **Agency in charge.** This column provides the name of the agency responsible for maintaining and/or publishing the data.
- **Data subject covered.** These columns indicate whether the data source covers specific data subjects. The data subjects are associated with freight transportation components (i.e., cargo or freight, vehicle or container, transportation network, and traffic control system), which are part of the freight data architecture described in this report.
- **Transportation mode covered.** These columns indicate whether the data source covers specific modes of freight transportation (i.e., air, rail, truck, water, and pipeline). Note that the combination between cargo (under data subject covered) and transportation mode provides an indication of the mode of transportation used to transport commodities.

It is worth noting that the list of freight data sources in Table 1 is primarily at the national level and is not comprehensive. In practice, state, regional, and local entities collect and maintain datasets such as truck counts, commercial vehicle inventory datasets, accident data, and facility data (e.g., data

Table 1. Freight-related data sources described in this report.

Freight Data Source/Dataset	Acronym	Agency in Charge	Data Subject Covered				Transportation Mode Covered				
			Cargo/Freight	Vehicle/Container	Transportation Network	Traffic Control System	Air	Rail	Truck	Water	Pipeline
Public Sector											
Agricultural Market Service Publications		U.S. Department of Agriculture (USDA) Agricultural Marketing Service	x				x	x	x	x	
Air Carrier Data		BTS		x			x				
Automated Commercial Environment/International Trade Data System	ACE/ITDS	U.S. Customs and Border Protection (CBP)	x	x			x	x	x	x	x
Automated Commercial System	ACS	CBP	x	x			x	x	x	x	
Automated Export System	AES	CBP	x	x			x		x	x	
Bureau of Labor Statistics (BLS) Databases		BLS	x				x	x	x	x	x
Bureau of Transportation Statistics Publications		BTS		x	x		x	x	x	x	x
Commodity Flow Survey	CFS	BTS, U.S. Census Bureau	x				x	x	x	x	
Economic Accounts (including the National Income and Product Accounts [NIPAs])		U.S. Bureau of Economic Analysis (BEA)					x	x	x	x	x
Economic Census		U.S. Census Bureau	x				x	x	x	x	
Energy Information Administration Data Services		Energy Information Administration	x		x			x	x		x
Fatality Analysis Reporting System	FARS	NHTSA		x					x		
Freight Analysis Framework	FAF2	FHWA	x		x		x	x	x	x	
Hazardous Materials Information System	HMIS	PHMSA	x	x			x	x	x	x	x
Highway Performance Monitoring System	HPMS	FHWA			x	x			x		
Motor Carrier Financial and Operating Data		FMCSA	x	x					x		
Motor Carrier Management Information System	MCMIS	FMCSA	x	x					x		
Motor Carrier Safety Status Measurement System	SafeStat	FMCSA		x					x		
National Automotive Sampling System	NASS	NHTSA		x					x		
National Hazardous Material Route Registry	NHMRR	FMCSA			x				x		
National Pipeline Mapping System	NPMS	PHMSA	x	x							x
National Transportation Atlas Database	NTAD	BTS			x	x	x	x	x	x	
Navigation Data Center Waterborne Commerce Data		U.S. Army Corps of Engineers (USACE)	x	x	x	x				x	
North American Transborder Freight Database		BTS	x				x	x	x	x	x
Railroad Data (including the Carload Waybill Sample)		Surface Transportation Board (STB)	x	x	x			x			
Service Annual Survey		U.S. Census Bureau	x	x					x		
Statistics Canada		Statistics Canada	x	x	x		x	x	x	x	x
Surface Transportation Board Economic Data and Tools		STB	x		x			x			
TradeStats Express		International Trade Administration	x				x	x	x	x	x
TranStats		BTS	x	x	x				x		
U.S. Census Bureau Foreign Trade Statistics		U.S. Census Bureau	x				x	x	x	x	x
Vehicle Travel Information System	VTRIS	FHWA		x					x		
Workforce Information Database	WID	States					x	x	x	x	x
Private Sector											
Association of American Railroads (AAR) Publications		AAR	x	x	x			x			
American Trucking Associations Monthly Reports		ATA		x					x		
Colography Group Services		Colography Group, Inc.	x				x		x		
IHS Global Insight Services		IHS Global Insight	x				x	x	x	x	x
Intermodal Association of North America Information Services		Intermodal Association of North America (IANA)	x	x				x	x	x	
Lloyd's MIU Services		Lloyd's MIU		x	x					x	

Table 1. (Continued).

Freight Data Source/Dataset	Acronym	Agency in Charge	Data Subject Covered				Transportation Mode Covered				
			Cargo/Freight	Vehicle/Container	Transportation Network	Traffic Control System	Air	Rail	Truck	Water	Pipeline
Port Import Export Reporting Service	PIERS	United Business Media (UBM) Global Trade	x		x					x	
State of Logistics Report		Council of Supply Chain Management Professionals (CSCMP)	x						x		
Worldwide Airport Traffic Reports		Airports Council International (ACI)	x				x				
Freight-Related Architectures, Frameworks, Programs, and Standards											
Commodity, Product, and Industry Classifications		Several	x				x	x	x	x	x
Electronic Data Interchange Standards	EDI	Several	x	x			x	x	x	x	x
National ITS Architecture		Research and Innovative Technology Administration (RITA)				x			x		
National Spatial Data Infrastructure	NSDI	Federal Geographic Data Committee (FGDC)			x	x	x	x	x	x	x
Initiatives under Development											
Electronic Freight Management	EFM	FHWA	x				x	x	x	x	
Freight Performance Measurement		FHWA			x				x		
Multimodal Hazmat Intelligence Portal	HIP	PHMSA	x		x		x	x	x	x	x

about ports, warehouses, and crossings). These datasets supplement national-level datasets. Likewise, Table 1 does not include data from trade associations, such as the National Industrial Transportation League (NITL) and the National Association of Retailers. Although the list does not include all of the potential data sources that deal with freight transportation, the list is useful because it provides a sample of the typical national-level data sources that may need to be evaluated in detail while building the national freight data architecture, as well as any potential system implementations that could be derived from that data architecture.

Readers should also note that some data sources in Table 1 might include multiple datasets. For compactness, the table does not disaggregate data sources into datasets. For example, Table 1 does not show all of the datasets associated with the National Transportation Atlas Database or that may be available through Statistics Canada.

Furthermore, relationships between freight data, data source, and business processes are too complex for a single table or diagram. The number of business processes that deal with freight transportation at any given point in time (ranging from planning to policymaking, operations, and emergency management) is huge. Providing a single table that illustrates all of the relationships between freight data and business processes would be impractical—if not impossible—to develop.

System and Architecture Review

The following systems and architectures in Table 1 were of particular interest because of the processes that led to their development:

- Automated Commercial Environment/International Trade Data System,
- Carload Waybill Sample,
- Commodity Flow Survey,
- Electronic Data Interchange Standards,
- Freight Analysis Framework,
- Highway Performance Monitoring System,
- National Income and Product Accounts,
- National ITS Architecture,
- National Spatial Data Infrastructure, and
- National Transportation Atlas Database.

Lessons learned from the development and implementation of these systems and architectures can provide invaluable information for, and help to minimize the costs of, the development and implementation of a national freight data architecture. This section presents a summary of the analysis completed on those systems and architectures. The analysis covered several topics, including the following:

- Purpose and intended benefits;
- Content;
- Institutional arrangements used for developing and maintaining the system or architecture;
- Challenges and issues faced in creating and maintaining the architecture or system;
- Strategies and methods for dealing with data integration issues, such as data quality, timeliness, and proprietary and privacy concerns;
- Adaptability to serve evolving purposes and data sources; and
- Assessment of how well the system or architecture works in the form of lessons learned.

In reality, institutional arrangements, issues faced during development, implemented strategies, and adaptability are interrelated. The reason is that, historically, systems tend to evolve and strategies are put in place not just to meet the goals and objectives of an initial master plan but also in response to challenges and issues faced during the implementation and/or maintenance phases of those systems. For convenience, to avoid redundancy in the presentation, and for readability purposes, each analysis in this section includes three subsections, as follows:

- Purpose and content;
- Development, challenges, strategies, and adaptability; and
- Lessons learned.

Automated Commercial Environment/International Trade Data System

Purpose and Content

ACE is a trade data processing system that CBP is implementing to support customs activities at U.S. borders (15). The ACE effort is a multi-year, multi-million-dollar project that is replacing the 1984 ACS legacy system.

ACE uses a secure data portal that enables the trade community and participating government agencies (PGAs) to connect to the ACE database as well as to legacy databases (Figure 5). ACE provides a single, centralized access point for communications and information related to cargo shipments. Through the portal, it is possible to manage accounts, perform periodic payments, enter data for electronic truck manifests (also called e-Manifests), and generate reports. E-Manifests enable tracking of crew, equipment, shipper, consignee, and shipment data. E-Manifests are now required when entering the country through any of the 99 land border ports of entry. CBP plans to extend ACE to provide cargo processing capabilities across all modes of transportation, replacing existing systems with a single, multimodal manifest system for land, air, rail, and sea cargo.

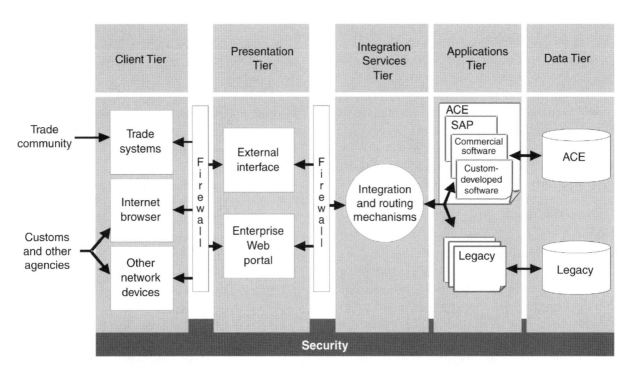

Figure 5. ACE framework (16).

ITDS is a federal program that encourages PGA participation in ACE (*17*). The program assists PGAs in identifying, documenting, and executing plans to improve business operations through their participation in ACE. Currently, 46 PGAs are involved in the ITDS program. Nearly 500 users from 27 PGAs have access to the ACE portal. One of the mechanisms the ITDS program uses to support the integration of PGAs into ACE is through the development of the ACE/ITDS standard dataset. This dataset is a collection of data requirements for international trade and U.S. border regulatory and enforcement processes. Its purpose is to ensure data harmonization to facilitate the full implementation of ACE across all relevant federal agencies. CBP is working to align the dataset with the international data standards developed by the World Customs Organization (WCO).

Development, Challenges, Strategies, and Adaptability

Critical milestones in the creation and development of ACE and ITDS are the following:

- In 1993, the U.S. Customs Service commissioned a report (*Future Automated Commercial Environment Team [FACET] Report*) to make recommendations for the redesign of its commercial processing systems.
- In 1994, a multi-agency task force composed of representatives of 53 agencies was formed to develop recommendations for implementing an international trade data system that could meet the needs of the federal government, business community, and public.
- In 1995, vice presidential memoranda chartered the ITDS Project Office in the Department of the Treasury as well as a multi-agency ITDS board of directors. Over time, this management structure has evolved to include committees, working groups, and integrated product teams, frequently with PGA participation.
- In 1998, formal design and concept of operations documents were prepared and a pilot system called the North American Trade Automation Prototype (NATAP) was approved to demonstrate the benefits of ITDS.
- In 2000, the ITDS Project Office was transferred to the U.S. Customs Service and its goals were refined to fit better into the U.S. Customs Service operational environment.
- In 2001, ACE started with an initial appropriation of $130 million (*18*). Development of ACE started the same year. In 2004, it was estimated that the full deployment of ACE would be completed by December 2007 at an estimated cost of $2.24 billion (*19*).
- In August 2001, the ITDS pilot project went live in Buffalo, NY. The pilot project was suspended the following month due to operational considerations at the port following the September 11, 2001, terrorist attacks.
- In 2003, the first ACE portal accounts were established.
- In 2003, the U.S. Customs Service moved to DHS and became U.S. Customs and Border Protection. Following this transition, the ITDS program focus changed to provide support to the integration of PGAs into ACE. As previously mentioned, one of the mechanisms to promote this integration is through the development of the ACE/ITDS standard dataset.
- In 2004, ACE e-Manifest was deployed in Blaine, WA (*20*). Since then, e-Manifest has been deployed at all 99 land border ports of entry. In 2006, CBP conducted an evaluation of the e-Manifest initiative (*21*). From surveys, site visits, and telephone interviews, the study found that using electronic manifests resulted in smoother border crossing operations, a lower number of secondary inspections, and a higher number of post-secondary inspections.

Developing the ACE/ITDS dataset was a significant challenge over a 2-year period, which involved compiling a list of data elements from PGAs, clarifying data element definitions required by each PGA, working with PGAs to identify and eliminate overlapping data requirements, and translating those data elements into specific software requirements while ensuring consistency with ACE (*22*). From the 10,000 data elements that PGAs identified, ACE/ITDS staff reduced the number of required data elements by 96 percent to a standard dataset of 400 data elements. CBP is also working to harmonize the ITDS standard dataset with the WCO data model.

As mentioned, 46 PGAs are currently involved in the ITDS program. Different PGAs are at different stages of ACE integration (*23*). Several U.S.DOT operating administrations plan to access CBP data through an interface between ACE and the U.S.DOT's planned International Freight Data System (IFDS) (*24*), with different levels of access depending on the statutory authority of each U.S.DOT operating administration. For example,

- BTS plans to use ACE data such as entry data from importers, manifest data from carriers, and carrier contact information from ACE carrier account tables to conduct a variety of statistical analyses.
- FHWA plans to access summary and manifest data to analyze cargo and conveyance movements in order to better allocate resources among states.
- FMCSA plans to access ACE data to analyze international truck freight flows in connection with enforcement activities and the allocation of federal resources among state motor carrier safety agencies. The interface between CBP and FMCSA is currently undergoing testing to analyze the

volume of screening issues and system screening performance. Over the next 2 years, various functions will be phased in, including screening of manifest information, notifications to carriers, and warnings to send vehicles to an FMCSA inspection facility.

RITA is the primary agency responsible for developing and managing IFDS.

Lessons Learned

Lessons learned in connection with the development, evolution, and maintenance of ACE and ITDS follow:

- **Develop robust implementation plan with adequate stakeholder involvement.** By all accounts, ACE has been a huge undertaking. Developing a brand new system to replace the myriad of ad hoc programs and procedures that have evolved for decades at Customs (while taking into consideration the needs of all affected stakeholders) is not a trivial task. Despite the magnitude and complexity of the project, CBP essentially relied on its external contractors during the development phase without ensuring adequate PGA participation. This lack of coordination affected the ACE/ITDS development process.
- **Clearly define expected outcomes and development and coordination plan.** The process to consolidate 10,000 data elements into a list of 400 data elements was highly iterative and required the involvement of a large number of stakeholders. Therefore, it was critical to identify the expected goals and outcomes as well as the procedures for coordination and data element conflict resolution. However, the process was not clearly defined, eventually resulting in two versions of the dataset. There also were issues related to dataset ownership and responsible-party designation to modify and/or add data elements.
- **Address needs of stakeholders.** Developing an accurate understanding of the data needs of affected stakeholders is an important project development requirement. For the development of the ACE/ITDS standard dataset, it was critical to properly document the needs of all the PGAs involved.

However, there were inconsistencies in the process, which resulted in some data needs not being properly identified.

Carload Waybill Sample

Purpose and Content

The Carload Waybill Sample is a stratified sample of carload waybills for terminated shipments at railroad carriers (*25*). STB is the agency responsible for the management of the Carload Waybill Sample. Railinc, Corp., a wholly-owned subsidiary of AAR, is under contract with STB for the production of the sample. The Carload Waybill Sample captures data about O-D points, number of carloads, tonnage, participating railroads, interchange locations, and total freight revenue. The sample is one of the main sources of information for the development of trip generation estimates and is often used by regulators, planners, nongovernmental agencies, and other stakeholders.

The sampling rate for carload waybill samples is a function of the number of carloads per waybill and the method the railroad uses to submit the documentation (i.e., manually or using a computerized system) (*25, 26*). Table 2 lists current sampling rate requirements. The vast majority of railroads submit sample data electronically. Because of the threshold for submission, the Carload Waybill Sample does not account for many Class II or III railroads. In 2007, there were 565 freight railroads in the United States, with only 63 freight railroads filing a sample of waybills (*27, 28*). The sample does not capture data from export shipments carried on Canadian railroads operating inside the United States. The Carload Waybill Sample has increased in size over the years, from 346,903 in 1986 to 666,989 in 2007 (*27*).

The stratified sample of carload waybills provides information about shipments by rail, including STCC codes, origins, and destinations. The sample results in two types of files as follows (*26*):

- **Master file.** The master file contains movement-specific confidential waybill data and is therefore limited to authorized users as required by Code of Federal Regulations (CFR) Title 49 Section 1244 (49 CFR 1244). Current regulations

Table 2. Carload waybill sampling rates (*25, 26*).

Reporting Method	Number of Carloads per Waybill	Expected Sampling Rate
Manual	15	1/100
Manual	625	1/10
Manual	26 and more	1/5
Computerized	12	1/40
Computerized	315	1/12
Computerized	1660	1/4
Computerized	61100	1/3
Computerized	101 and more	1/2

for use of the master file pertain to the protection of specific shipper or carrier data that are considered proprietary. The master file includes 176 data items.

- **Public use file.** The public use file is an aggregated, less detailed file that contains non-confidential data and is available to the public without restrictions. This file removes several fields to shield confidential data and provides the data in a geographically aggregated manner. The public use data file includes 63 data items.

Development, Challenges, Strategies, and Adaptability

Shipper freight movement data have been collected and analyzed since the late 1800s (27). The Interstate Commerce Commission (ICC) was responsible for these data until 1995, when it was replaced by STB. The Carload Waybill Sample has been continuously collected since 1946. As required in 49 CFR 1241-1248, railroads must submit reports to document their operations to STB (26), as follows:

- 49 CFR 1241 requires Class I railroads to submit annual financial data, covering elements such as total revenue, inventory of equipment, track and traffic conditions, and mileage (26, 29).
- 49 CFR 1243 requires Class I railroads to submit quarterly reports documenting revenues, expenses, income, fuel costs, fuel consumption, and fuel surcharges.
- 49 CFR 1244 requires railroads terminating at least 4,500 cars per year or that transport at least 5 percent of any state's total traffic to submit carload waybill samples. Railroads must submit waybill samples at least quarterly. These samples are the basis for the STB Carload Waybill Sample (25, 26).
- 49 CFR 1245 requires Class I railroads to submit quarterly and annual reports of railroad employees, service, and compensation.
- 49 CFR 1246 requires Class I railroads to submit monthly reports of the number of railroad employees.
- 49 CFR 1248 requires Class I railroads to submit quarterly and annual freight commodity statistics using CCTS codes issued by the Bureau of the Budget (i.e., the predecessor of the Office of Management and Budget [OMB]). Railroads must report on a number of data elements for each commodity code, including revenue, number of carloads, and tonnage. Railroads also must report on the average number of miles operated and gross freight revenue.

In addition, as required by 49 CFR 225, all railroads regardless of size must submit safety reports to FRA (30).

As previously mentioned, the Carload Waybill Sample is one of the main sources of information for the development of trip generation estimates and is often used by regulators, planners,

nongovernmental agencies, and other stakeholders. The sample is also used for the calculation of the Rail Cost Adjustment Factor (RCAF), which measures the rate of inflation in railroad inputs such as labor and fuel and is therefore used to determine shipment rate adjustments (31, 32). AAR submits all of the RCAF components to STB for review and approval, first as a forecast and then actual data two quarters later.

Lessons Learned

Lessons learned in connection with the development, evolution, and maintenance of the Carload Waybill Sample follow:

- **Provide clear, uniform guidance.** The regulations clearly identify which freight railroads are required to submit a Carload Waybill Sample. They also clearly state who is eligible to receive the data and the restrictions for those parties in which to use the data. In addition, both STB and Railinc have developed several documents that assist railroads in the understanding of the reporting requirements.
- **Develop mechanisms that facilitate use of data for various purposes but also maintain necessary confidentiality.** The Carload Waybill Sample data are both necessary and desired by a variety of users. The guiding regulations clearly define five classes of users of the data and statutory requirements for each group to use the data. This regulation is designed to maintain confidentiality of the data while also providing critical information. Relevance of the data is also maintained by the role that Railinc plays, which includes collecting and processing data on behalf of the railroads and submitting the data collected to STB. Railinc also provides real-time data exchange services to the railroad industry.

Commodity Flow Survey

Purpose and Content

CFS is a joint effort between the U.S. Census Bureau and BTS to gather and compile data on the movement of goods in the United States (33–36). CFS is a shipper-based survey that gathers data from shipments in the United States. With the exception of operating status and the verification of name and location, CFS does not collect data on shipper or receiver descriptors. CFS includes the following shipment data:

- Shipment ID number, date, value, and weight;
- SCTG commodity code;
- Commodity description;
- Destination (and port of exit in the case of exports);
- Mode(s) of transportation;
- Mode of export; and
- Hazardous material (hazmat) code.

CFS collects shipment data from a sample of establishments selected from the U.S. Census Bureau Business Register. These establishments are from manufacturing, mining, wholesale, select retail and service industries (electronic shopping, mail-order houses, and fuel dealers), and auxiliary establishments (i.e., warehouses and managing offices) of multi-establishment companies. CFS does not include establishments from the following industries: crude petroleum and natural gas extraction, farms, government establishments, trans-border shipments, imports (until the shipment reaches the first domestic shipper), and remaining service industries. Many of these industries (e.g., farms and government establishments) are not included in the Business Register. Each establishment selected is mailed a questionnaire four times during the year. For each questionnaire, the establishment provides specific data about a sample of individual outbound shipments during a pre-specified 1-week period.

CFS data are available at several levels of geographic resolution, such as national, state, metropolitan area, and census regions and divisions. Key statistics from CFS include the following:

- Value, tons, ton miles, average miles per shipment;
- Commodity shipped;
- Modes of transportation; and
- O-D flows.

CFS data are used to assess demand on existing transportation systems and assist with critical investments in future transportation facilities and services. For example, CFS data are used to build truck O-D trip tables, for traffic simulation analyses, to benchmark the Carload Waybill Sample (37), and as input to the Freight Analysis Framework. Commercial databases such as TRANSEARCH® Insight also use CFS data.

Development, Challenges, Strategies, and Adaptability

CFS is a component of the 5-year U.S. Census Bureau's Economic Census. It was first conducted in 1993. Between 1963 and 1977, information about commodities transported in the United States was collected through a survey of American businesses as part of the economic census. However, due to data reliability issues, this survey was last published in 1977 (38). Data reliability problems also affected a smaller commodity transportation study in 1983, which caused the U.S. Census Bureau not to publish the results (38). In 1991, a TRB report identified the lack of commodity flow data as one of the greatest gaps in the U.S.DOT data program (39). Following its creation that year, BTS instituted CFS and arranged with the U.S. Census Bureau to conduct the survey as part of

the economic census (38). BTS provides 80 percent of the funding, while the U.S. Census Bureau provides the remaining 20 percent (35).

CFS has been conducted four times, as follows:

- In 1993, the CFS sample size was about 200,000 establishments based on a Standard Industrial Classification (SIC) stratification. The 1993 CFS used STCC codes. The budget for the 1993 CFS was $15 million.
- In 1997, the CFS sample size was reduced to about 100,000 establishments based on a SIC-based industry group stratification. The response rate was 75 percent. The 1997 CFS used SCTG codes. The reporting period was reduced to 1 week (from 2 weeks required in the 1993 CFS). The budget for the 1997 CFS was $19 million.
- In 2002, the CFS sample size was reduced to about 50,000 establishments based on a North American Industry Classification System (NAICS) stratification. The response rate was about 70 percent. The 2002 CFS used SCTG codes. The budget for the 2002 CFS was $13 million.
- In 2007, the CFS sample size was increased to about 100,000 establishments based on an NAICS-based stratification. The 2007 CFS used SCTG codes.

Although CFS is widely used for a variety of applications, it has some limitations, including the following (35, 37):

- **Gaps in shipment and industry coverage.** CFS does not collect shipment data for certain industries and commodities, and does not collect shipment data for shipments passing through the United States. In addition, cross-border shipment paths only include U.S. mileage. According to a 2002 estimate, non-CFS shipments were 36 percent by value, about 40 percent by tonnage, and about 29 percent by ton-miles (36). Further, the survey does not capture route information beyond shipper and receiver locations, which makes estimating intermodal drayage components difficult. In general, intermodal freight volumes may be low due to the CFS definition of "intermodal."
- **Lack of geographic and commodity detail at the state and local levels.** There is widespread agreement that increased geographic and commodity detail at the state and local levels would greatly enhance the usefulness of the survey. The challenge is how to determine the optimum level of disaggregation. Geographic strata for the 1993 and 1997 CFSs included 89 national transportation analysis regions (NTARs). These regions were consolidated 1987 BEA economic areas to keep O-D tables within 8,000 cells. Geographic strata in the 2002 CFS included the top 50 metropolitan areas (MAs) based on population in the 2000 Census, with establishments not located in an MA

assigned to the remainder of the state. Geographic strata in the 2007 CFS will use 73 MAs, with establishments not located in an MA assigned to the remainder of the state. Several ideas have been suggested to increase CFS regions, including using three-digit zip code regions (of which there are 929 around the country) and BEA areas (of which there are 172 around the country) (37). A recent study of techniques to generate national freight analysis zones (FAZs) for transportation models recommended a system of 400 zones (40).

- **Insensitivity to short-term economic changes.** CFS follows a 5-year cycle, which is inadequate for freight analyses in connection with phenomena such as recessions or droughts. The 2-year lag between data collection and release of results is also a weakness.

Lessons Learned

Lessons learned in connection with the development, evolution, and maintenance of CFS follow:

- **Continue to involve the U.S. Census Bureau for the use of survey instruments.** CFS is a joint effort between the U.S. Census Bureau and BTS. According to BTS, this partnership has been beneficial because the U.S. Census Bureau had previous experience conducting commodity-based surveys, an establishment list, and in-house resources for data collection (37).
- **Create crosswalks to ensure the compatibility of survey data internally over time and externally across other datasets.** Over time, key CFS characteristics have changed, such as sample size, industry classification, commodity classification, survey methodology, and data items. A documented crosswalk between CFS surveys to link survey data over time is needed (37). In addition, while CFS is a shipment survey, other surveys that can be used to supplement CFS data (e.g., carrier surveys) contain data that are not necessarily compatible with the CFS data structure. There is also a need for an integrated data collection program and coordination on definitions for commodity codes and vehicle types (37).
- **Consider importance of adequate resources for data collection and fully understanding implications of small sample sizes.** Due to delays and limited funding, the 2002 CFS design made limited use of prior surveys and did not incorporate pilot studies (37). The sample size also was reduced from 100,000 to 50,000 establishments, which degraded the quality and usefulness of the data. There also were communication issues such as not sharing sampling procedures and relevant documentation with CFS data users (35).

Electronic Data Interchange Standards

Purpose and Content

EDI standards are data exchange standards that facilitate the exchange and interpretation of formatted data messages between computers. EDI formatted data messages are business documents, examples of which include rate proposals, invoices, purchase orders, and ship notices. The two parties in an EDI transaction are usually called trading partners. Although the term EDI can be used in connection with any formatted exchange of data between computers, EDI frequently applies to the standards developed by the American National Standards Institute Accredited Standards Committee (ANSI ASC) X12 (41). Other formatted data exchange standards used by the freight community include the following:

- United Nations Electronic Data Interchange for Administration, Commerce, and Transport (UN/EDIFACT) standards (42). These standards are predominant outside of North America.
- Universal Business Language (UBL) (43). UBL is a library of standard extensible markup language (XML) electronic business documents developed by the Organization for the Advancement of Structured Information Standards (OASIS), which is an international non-profit organization that seeks the adoption of open interoperability standards for business applications.

Federal Information Processing Standards Publication (FIPS PUB) 1612 describes the requirements to use EDI standards within the federal government (44).

ANSI ASC X12 standards define data message (or transaction set) components such as message syntax, message type, control data elements, data segments, message grouping, and message authentication. A transaction set is divided into data segments, where a segment is a collection of data elements that typically includes a segment ID, data elements separated by delimiters, and a segment terminator. A segment within a transaction set can be mandatory, optional, or conditional. Many transaction sets have three parts: header (which starts with a header segment), detail, and summary (which ends with a trailer segment).

ANSI ASC X12 has sponsored the development of more than 300 EDI standard transaction sets (and, increasingly, XML schemas) in a wide range of areas such as materials, warehousing, product services, and transportation. Many EDI transaction sets are related to freight and cover topics such as rate proposals, freight details and invoices, trailer manifests, shipment information, shipment status inquiries and status messages, and tariff information. Table 3 lists a short sample of freight-related ANSI ASC X12 transaction sets.

26

Table 3. Sample of freight-related ANSI ASC X12 transaction sets.

No.	Description
104	Air Shipment Information
109	Vessel Content Details
110	Air Freight Details and Invoice
210	Motor Carrier Freight Details and Invoice
211	Motor Carrier Bill of Lading
214	Transportation Carrier Shipment Status Message
215	Motor Carrier Pick-up Manifest
216	Motor Carrier Shipment Pick-up Notification
217	Motor Carrier Loading and Route Guide
218	Motor Carrier Tariff Information
309	Customs Manifest
310	Freight Receipt and Invoice (Ocean)
311	Canadian Customs Information
315	Status Details (Ocean)
319	Terminal Information
322	Terminal Operations and Intermodal Ramp Activity
323	Vessel Schedule and Itinerary (Ocean)
350	U.S. Customs Status Information
353	U.S. Customs Events Advisory Details
404	Rail Carrier Shipment Information
410	Rail Carrier Freight Details and Invoice
426	Rail Revenue Waybill
435	Standard Transportation Commodity Code Master
437	Railroad Junctions and Interchanges Activity
440	Shipment Weights
451	Railroad Event Report
470	Railroad Clearance
601	U.S. Customs Export Shipment Information
715	Intermodal Group Loading Plan
853	Routing and Carrier Instruction
857	Shipment and Billing Notice
858	Shipment Information
859	Freight Invoice

Development, Challenges, Strategies, and Adaptability

Significant milestones in the development of the ASC X12 standards include the following (41):

- In 1979, ANSI formed Accredited Standards Committee X12 to develop uniform standards for electronic exchange of business transactions.
- In 1982, ANSI published Version 1 of the American National Standards. Over the years, ANSI has published revised versions of these standards, which are ANSI-certified releases of draft ASC X12 standards.
- In 1986, project teams were formed as precursors to functional subcommittees. Currently, ASC X12 has seven subcommittees (communications and control, finance, government, insurance, supply chain, technical assessment, and transportation) as well as several task groups.
- In 1990, an alignment task group was formed to recommend steps to converge ASC X12 standards and EDIFACT messages.

- In 1999, an XML task group was formed to draft policies and procedures related to EDI and XML.
- In 2000, the Health Insurance Portability and Accountability Act (HIPAA) transaction regulation (45 CFR 160 and 162) was published adopting nine ASC X12 transaction sets for the health care industry (45). ASC X12 signed a memorandum of understanding (MOU) with the Department of Health and Human Services and standards development organizations to manage the EDI standards adopted under HIPAA.
- In 2001, ASC X12 and the UN/EDIFACT working group started work to create a single set of core components that could work on both standards environments.
- In 2005, ASC X12 published the first set of XML schemas.

Although EDI standards are independent of hardware and software communication technologies, EDI implementations typically require the use of special-purpose software for the transmission and interpretation of EDI transaction sets. Traditional EDI implementations use direct modem-to-modem connections. However, the number of EDI implementations that use Web-based communication protocols (e.g., hypertext transfer protocol over secure socket layer [HTTPS] and Applicability Statement [AS]), is increasing rapidly. Many implementations rely on value-added networks (VANs) to facilitate communications between trading partners.

There are several versions and releases of the ANSI ASC X12 standards (e.g., 3040, 4010, 5010, and 6010). EDI applications are normally built upon specific version releases. Different releases are not compatible, which adds complexity to the data exchange process. The decision to upgrade an EDI application to a more recent version of the standard depends on a number of factors, including cost to upgrade and what versions are used by current and potential trading partners. In large companies, it is common to have internal technical teams that support the development and maintenance of in-house applications. In smaller companies, it is more common to outsource EDI communications to third-party vendors. The alternative to upgrading is to purchase EDI translation software (which often costs in excess of $50,000) or contract with third parties to translate data formats, data elements, and qualifiers to ensure compatibility with the EDI standard versions required by trading partners in the supply chain.

The disparities between different versions of EDI standards currently in use may at least partially explain why many supply chain stakeholders either build their own systems to the minimum "mandatory" specifications and omit the more robust ("optional") data elements or outsource EDI data exchange to a third-party provider.

To address some of the limitations associated with traditional EDI transaction sets (including proprietary software implementations, cryptic format, and implementation complexity), ASC X12 developed a Context Inspired Component Architecture (CICA) that enables the construction of XML-based message sets that rely on reusable vocabulary across multiple industries (*41*). In CICA, data element definitions (e.g., date, time, and name) are XML constructs that can be reused multiple times as needed. ASC X12 has published a number of XML schemas, including the following, which are related to transportation:

- Transportation freight invoice,
- Transportation status—general use,
- Transportation status—small package use,
- Transportation status—general use request,
- Transportation empty car release—rail request,
- Transportation empty car release—rail response, and
- Transportation price distribution—rail.

Commodity, Product, and Industry Classification Standards

As previously mentioned, many EDI transactions sets are related to freight. Of particular interest are transaction sets that provide information about the commodities being transported. For motor carrier shipments, ANSI ASC X12 Transaction Set 211 describes commodity items using national motor freight classification (NMFC) codes. NMFC is a standard maintained by the National Motor Freight Traffic Association (NMFTA) that groups commodities into 18 classes according to four commodity "transportability" characteristics: density, stowability, handling, and liability (*46*).

NMFC is one of several commodity and product classification standards available to the freight community. Widely known standards include the following:

- **Central Product Classification (CPC).** CPC is a product classification system sponsored by the United Nations, which uses a five-digit hierarchical structure that provides three levels of product code resolution (*47*). With some exceptions, CPC subclasses are groupings and rearrangements of Harmonized System (HS) codes. CPC code listings provide an indication of the corresponding HS codes, along with International Standard Industrial Classification (ISIC) activity classes (*47*). CPC provides the base for the Standards Nomenclature for Transport Statistics (NST 2007) classification system (*48*).
- **Harmonized System.** HS is an international product coding system developed by the WCO (*49*). HS uses a six-digit hierarchical structure that provides three levels of commodity code resolution. Most countries have adopted HS, including the United States, which used HS as the basis for the Harmonized Tariff Schedule (HTS) maintained by the U.S. International Trade Commission (USITC) (*50*).

- **National Motor Freight Classification.** As previously mentioned, NMFC groups commodities into 18 classes according to four commodity "transportability" characteristics: density, stowability, handling, and liability (*46*). the access and use of NMFC codes is limited by 49 U.S. Code Section 13703 (49 USC 13703) to specific regulated carriers (*51, 52*).
- **North American Product Classification System (NAPCS).** NAPCS is a product classification system the United States, Canada, and Mexico are developing to complement NAICS (*53*).
- **Price Look-Up (PLU).** PLU codes are used by the produce sector to describe products such as fruits, vegetables, dried fruit, herbs and flavorings, and nuts (*54*). Typically, sealed, containerized, or packaged produce falls outside the scope of the PLU coding system. Also excluded is produce that has undergone additional processing.
- **Standard Classification of Transported Goods.** SCTG codes are commodity codes that were developed to support the needs of the 1997 CFS (*55*). SCTG uses a five-digit hierarchical structure that aggregates HS codes into categories that CFS planners considered more suitable for statistical analyses and the collection of freight movement data.
- **Standard Transportation Commodity Codes.** STCCs are commodity codes used by the railroad industry to describe product information in waybills and other shipping documents. AAR developed STCC in 1962 using a seven-digit structure that provided five levels of commodity code resolution (*56*). It may be worth noting that CFS shifted from STCC to SCTG codes in 1997. As a result, other applications that rely on CFS data (such as FAF) also changed to SCTG (*57*).

Most of the product classification standards above provide a mapping of product codes to industrial classification systems such as the following:

- **International Standard Industrial Classification of All Economic Activities.** ISIC classifies industries using a four-digit hierarchical structure that provides three levels of industry code resolution (*47*). At the top level, the two-digit division codes are grouped into sections designated by letters (which are not included in the ISIC codes).
- **North American Industry Classification System.** NAICS classifies industries using a six-digit hierarchical structure that provides six levels of industry code resolution (*58*). NAICS replaced SIC in 1997.
- **Standard Industrial Classification.** SIC classified industries using a four-digit hierarchical structure that provided four levels of industry code resolution (*59*). SIC has been replaced by NAICS and is no longer in use by the federal government.

28

Examples of crosswalk tables that enable the mapping of codes across systems include the following:

- Five-digit CPC codes and six-digit HS codes (*47*),
- Five-digit CPC codes and four-digit ISIC codes (*47*),
- Two-digit HS codes and two-digit SCTG codes (*57*),
- Two-digit SCTG codes and four-digit STCC codes (*57*),
- Six-digit NAICS codes and four-digit SIC codes (*58*), and
- Four-digit ISIC codes and six-digit NAICS codes (*60*).

It is worth noting that crosswalk tables are actually snapshot views because they use specific versions of the corresponding codes linked by the crosswalk tables. Crosswalk table maintenance practices vary widely from agency to agency. In addition, there is no centralized repository of links to current and historical crosswalk tables.

Readers also should be aware that the list of classification standards provided above is only a sample. Additional classification standards that should be taken into consideration for the development of a national freight data architecture include the following:

- HMIS regulations and classification standards,
- Federal and state vehicle type/class classification standards,
- Vessel classification standards,
- Railcar classification standards, and
- Facility classifications.

Lessons Learned

Lessons learned in connection with the development, evolution, and maintenance of EDI standards follow:

- **Develop applications that rely on widely used data standards.** The ANSI ASC X12 EDI standards have been around for almost 30 years and are widely used in industries such as retail, transportation, education, health care, travel, and insurance. Many EDI transactions sets are related to freight and cover topics such as rate proposals, freight details and invoices, trailer manifests, shipment information, shipment status inquiries and status messages, and tariff information. Traditional EDI implementations use direct modem-to-modem connections. However, the number of EDI implementations that use Web-based communication protocols (e.g., HTTPS and AS) is increasing rapidly. To support this transition, ASC X12 is beginning to develop XML schemas, which facilitate data exchange using modern communication technologies.
- **Develop applications with backward compatibility.** There are several versions and releases of the ANSI ASC X12 standards (e.g., 3040, 4010, 5010, and 6010). EDI applications are normally built upon specific version releases. Unfortu-

nately, different releases are not compatible, which adds complexity to the data exchange process. The disparities between different versions of EDI standards currently in use may at least partially explain why many supply chain stakeholders either build their own systems to the minimum "mandatory" specifications and omit the more robust ("optional") data elements or outsource EDI data exchange to a third-party provider.

- **Participate in the standards development process.** For motor carrier shipments, ANSI ASC X12 Transaction Set 211 describes commodity items using NMFC codes. NMFC is a standard maintained by NMFTA, which groups commodities into 18 classes according to four commodity "transportability" characteristics: density, stowability, handling, and liability. NMFC codes are not compatible with other commodity classification codes commonly used by the freight community. Active participation by other freight stakeholders in the development of ASC X12 standards would be an effective mechanism to help address code incompatibility problems.

Freight Analysis Framework

Purpose and Content

FAF is a commodity O-D database and analytical framework that provides estimates of tonnage and values of goods shipped according to origin, destination, commodity, and mode (*57, 61*). In addition to commodity O-D data, FAF provides estimates of commodity movements by truck and volumes of long-distance trucks over specific highways. FAF was originally developed as a policy analysis tool within the U.S.DOT. Over time, FAF products have also used to convey freight profile and statistics to the states and the public, and as a tool to support economic analyses that involve commodity flow trends in areas other than transportation. Additional examples of FAF applications are documented in reports such as the *Quick Response Freight Manual* (*62*).

FAF includes 138 origin and destination "zones," consisting of 114 regions as defined in the 2002 CFS, 17 international gateways (which supplement FAF regions that are both gateways and domestic zones), and 7 international regions. Commodities are defined at the two-digit SCTG level. Although the 2002 CFS defines 11 separate modes, multimodal combinations, and unknown modes, FAF only uses 7 aggregated modes. FAF relies primarily on data collected every 5 years as part of the economic census.

Conceptually, the database of origins and destinations in FAF can be thought of as a four-dimensional matrix of origins, destinations, commodities, and modes, in which each cell in the four-dimensional matrix represents tonnage or value of goods shipped (*57*). The actual implementation of

FAF uses a database composed of several tables (63), including the following:

- **Domestic tonnage and value tables.** These tables contain the following data:
  - Origin: one of the 114 FAF/CFS domestic regions,
  - Origin state: state where the FAF origin region is located,
  - Destination: one of the 114 domestic regions,
  - Destination state: state where the FAF destination region is located,
  - Commodity: one of the 43 SCTG commodities,
  - Mode: one of the 7 aggregated modes, and
  - Years 2002–2035: thousand tons or million dollars for each year.
- **International tonnage and value tables.** These tables (for transborder, sea, and transocean air) contain the following data:
  - Origin: one of the 7 international regions (for imports) or one of the 114 domestic regions (for exports),
  - Origin state: state or international region where the FAF origin region is located,
  - Destination: one of the 7 international regions (for imports) or one of the 114 domestic regions (for exports),
  - Destination state: state or international region where the FAF destination region is located,
  - Commodity: one of the 43 SCTG commodities,
  - Port: one of the 17 international gateways,
  - Mode: one of the 7 aggregated modes used for the domestic portion of the movement, and
  - Years 2002–2035: thousand tons or million dollars for each year.

Development, Challenges, Strategies, and Adaptability

FAF versions include the following:

- **FAF1 (or "original" FAF).** This version of FAF, released in 2000, includes commodity O-D data for base year 1998 and future years 2010 and 2020. FAF1 relied partly on proprietary data.
- **FAF2 version 2.1 (FAF[2.1]).** This version of FAF, released in January 2006, includes commodity O-D data for base year 2002.
- **FAF2 version 2.2 (FAF[2.2]).** This version of FAF, released in November 2006, includes commodity O-D data for base year 2002 and future years 2010 through 2035 at 5-year intervals. Version 2.2 includes minor corrections to 2002 base year flows in Version 2.1. FAF2 also includes provisional data. Because the movement of goods may experience shifts between economic census years, FHWA produces provisional estimates of goods movement by origin,

destination, and mode, using publicly available publications that are less complete and detailed than the data used for the 2002 base estimate. The most recent year for which there are O-D estimates is 2007.

- **FAF2 version 2.3 (FAF[2.3]).** FAF[2.3], scheduled for release in 2009, will be the final version of the FAF2 series (64). This version will include minor adjustments to the 2002 O-D database, a distance matrix for estimating ton-miles, major corrections to the 1997 historical O-D file, and a Web-based tool for creating tables and extracting portions of the O-D database.
- **FAF3.** FHWA is currently working on FAF version 3 (FAF3) (64). FHWA anticipates releasing FAF3.0 by mid 2010, including the 2007 O-D commodity flow database, the 2007 highway network database, and initial ton-mile estimates by state. FHWA also expects to release FAF3.1 by the end of 2010 with forecasts, the rail and waterway network databases, and detailed ton-mile estimates. The current plan is to use FAF2 to release provisional 2008 and 2009 estimates (in 2009 and 2010, respectively) and use FAF3 to release 2010 provisional estimates (released in 2011) and other future years.

FAF1 was developed as a policy analysis tool within the U.S.DOT. FAF1 products were also used to convey freight profile and statistics to the states and the public, and as a tool to support economic analyses that involved commodity flow trends in areas other than transportation. However, FAF1's shortcomings, including its reliance on proprietary data and little use of CFS data, resulted in inconsistencies between FAF1 and CFS and the inability to publish estimates of commodity flows for areas smaller than states (64). A 2004 FHWA report identified improvement needs in areas related to geographic detail, completeness, accuracy, and timeliness (65). The 2004 report also outlined six goals for FAF2, as follows (64, 65):

1. Integrate economic census data more effectively,
2. Assure quality of FAF data for the benchmark years,
3. Provide timely updates to FAF data products,
4. Assure that FAF methods and products are transparent and can be reproduced,
5. Help state and local governments make effective use of FAF products in conjunction with developing a local understanding of freight activity, and
6. Continue to work with customers to improve the usefulness of FAF products.

Specific changes in FAF2 to meet these goals included the following:

- **Modes of transportation.** FAF2 was expanded to include all modes of transportation, including truck, rail, water, air, and pipeline. The term "intermodal" in FAF1 was based on CFS definitions, which include postal and courier shipments as well as any shipment using more than one mode of transportation. This definition was broader than other industry definitions such as trailer on flatcar or container on flatcar. As a result, FAF2 included two categories of "intermodal" shipments: truck-rail and other.

- **Commodity classification.** FAF2 changed from STCC to SCTG to address limitations in the STCC coding structure and to ensure consistency with critical data sources in FAF2 (particularly CFS).
- **Timeliness.** FHWA began releasing provisional estimates to address requests for more frequent updates than once every 5 years (when CFS occurs).
- **Public versus commercial data.** FAF2 shifted from using commercial, proprietary data to public data to populate its models because of limitations in FAF1 (which relied on commercial data) that prevented the publication of all FAF data. Disseminating all data in FAF2 was a strategy to enhance transparency, credibility, and public access.

Some of the issues raised in the 2004 report that FAF2 did not address but are relevant for FAF3 include the following (64):

- **Geographic region coverage and resolution.** FAF2 used 2002 CFS geographic regions. Because the number of geographic regions in CFS has increased since the 2002 census, updated CFS regions will be used for the 2007 benchmark O-D commodity flows, annual provisional estimates, and forecasts through 2040. FAF2 also excluded freight movements that passed through the United States. A strategy being considered is to use the North American Transportation Statistics Interchange forum, which includes the United States, Canada, and Mexico, to estimate in-transit flows at the national level.

  FAF2 includes a temporary file that contains disaggregated county-to-county commodity flows. However, FHWA does not publish the temporary file because of the large errors that result from disaggregating flows from regions to counties. With the increase in the number of CFS geographic regions, FHWA is considering options such as developing a standard region-to-county disaggregation method coupled with a program to collect supplemental data locally.

- **Transportation network coverage and resolution.** FAF2 relies mainly on National Highway Planning Network (NHPN) routes for assigning O-D commodity flows to the transportation network. FAF2 does not map freight movements that are shorter than 50 mi to this highway network. It also does not map commodity flows to individual rail lines, waterways, or pipelines. As in FAF1, FAF2 disaggregates flows to counties and selected sub-county generators

such as major ports, and then assigns the flows to routes. The process included matching route assignments to HPMS truck volume estimates, which revealed quality problems with HPMS data.

- **Temporal resolution.** FAF2 provides annual commodity flows. It does not handle seasonal, daily, or hourly variations in commodity flows. In addition, highway network assignment estimates are for peak period conditions. FAF2 simulates routing changes in response to bad weather by adjusting network impedances. A strategy that FHWA might consider is to use observed data from the Freight Performance Measurement initiative.
- **Modes of transportation.** FAF2 uses multimodal CFS definitions, which include shipments by postal and courier services and shipments that use more than one mode. This categorization is broader than trailer-on-flatcar or containerized service. FHWA is evaluating whether modal definitions can be developed within the confines of the 2007 CFS.
- **Shipper and carrier costs.** Forecasting costs and evaluating potential responses from the private sector, particularly shippers and carriers, requires access to transportation cost data. However, the collection of transportation cost data was largely discontinued after deregulation, and viable strategies have not been defined for obtaining this type of data in the future.
- **Feedback.** The FAF development team is small, which limits its capacity to respond to user requests and feedback. To address this limitation, FAF3 will include enhanced outreach methods to improve access to, and ease of use of, FAF products.

Lessons Learned

Lessons learned in connection with the development, evolution, and maintenance of FAF follow:

- **Use available data sources while keeping the system flexible to respond to changes and new data sources.** FAF was designed around existing information, particularly CFS, which, at the time of the FAF development, was one of the most comprehensive data sources available. FAF used CFS definitions of mode and geographic resolution and adapted other data sources to fill gaps in the CFS data. In the beginning, FAF used STCC codes. Eventually, FHWA changed to SCTG codes in order to address limitations in the STCC coding structure and to ensure consistency with critical data sources in FAF2, particularly CFS.
- **Develop systems that are consistent with input data limitations.** FAF's geographic region definitions are based on CFS region definitions. It would have been difficult, costly, and time consuming for FHWA to develop a much more

detailed region definition for FAF (e.g., at the county level) because, realistically, FHWA was not in a position to conduct a separate data collection effort to bypass CFS. By redefining those geographic regions, the quality of the FAF data would have suffered because the new commodity flow data would have relied much more on synthetic data instead of actual CFS data.

- **Implement strategies that promote adequate data access and transparency.** FHWA published not just FAF data products online but also ample documentation about the process to develop those products. Relying on proprietary data for the production of FAF1 prevented FHWA from publishing some of the FAF1 data products. This limitation was solved in FAF2 by relying mainly on public data.
- **Keep in mind the value of customer feedback.** FAF evolved from being a freight policy analysis tool into a product that is widely used by the freight community because new FAF releases took into consideration lessons learned from the use of the previous versions, including user feedback.

Highway Performance Monitoring System

Purpose and Content

HPMS is a system that contains data about the extent, condition, performance, use, and operating characteristics of the U.S. highway network (66). HPMS data are used for a variety of applications, including the following:

- Providing input to the production of reports to Congress on the condition, performance, and investment needs of U.S. highways, which Congress uses to establish authorization and appropriation legislation that affects the scope and size of the federal-aid highway program;
- Assessing changes in highway system performance and for apportioning federal-aid highway funds to individual states;
- Assembling freight corridors and determining freight movement performance;
- Special policy and planning studies;
- Travel and congestion monitoring, public road usage, and fatality rate calculations;
- Investment needs and planning at the state level; and
- Air quality conformance and planning.

Various agencies use HPMS data, including federal, state, and local agencies, as well as research agencies.

HPMS relies on annual data from state DOTs. The HPMS field manual (67) provides guidelines to state DOTs on the procedures to obtain and report data to HPMS, including precision levels and sample size estimation procedures. HPMS includes limited data on all public roads; detailed data on a sample of the arterial and collector functional systems;

and area-wide summary information for urbanized, small urban, and rural areas; as follows (Table 4) (67, 68):

- "Universe" data include basic inventory data on all open public road systems in the HPMS database. The basic inventory includes 46 data items for National Highway System (NHS) sections and 28 data items for local roads.
- "Sample" data include 98 data items containing additional inventory, condition, use, pavement, operational, and improvement data for 120,000 sections of roadway selected as standard samples.
- "Summary" data provide travel data for all functional systems in urbanized areas, small urban areas, and rural areas, as well as air quality non-attainment and maintenance areas.

In addition to other HPMS data, each state is required to submit linear referencing system (LRS) data in one of the following three category options: (1) maps and computer files, (2) LRSEDIT files and maps for new links and nodes, or (3) geographic information system (GIS) files. The HPMS field manual details these options (67). State-submitted LRS data are integrated with NHPN and are now published as part of NTAD in Environmental Systems Research Institute (ESRI™) shapefile format (see the National Transportation Atlas Database section in this chapter for additional information).

Development, Challenges, Strategies, and Adaptability

HPMS began in 1978 as a mechanism to replace annual data reports and biennial special studies that states conducted for FHWA (68). The special studies were in response to a 1965 requirement to produce a condition and performance (C&P) report on the nation's highways every 2 years. The first C&P report was completed in 1968. FHWA used data from state annual reports and biennial special studies, and subsequently has continued to use data from HPMS to produce the C&P reports mandated by Congress.

Federal legislation has continued the requirement for biennial reports, for example through the 1991 ISTEA (69); the 1998 TEA-21 (70); and the 2005 SAFETEA-LU (71). ISTEA introduced a requirement to provide the necessary information to enable the comparison of measures when these measures change. TEA-21 moved the report requirements from 23 USC 307 to 23 USC 502.

FHWA has modified HPMS several times to accommodate changes in legislation, technology, national priorities, and reporting requirements (72). For example

- In 1980, HPMS was merged with the Mileage Facilities Reporting System (MFRS), which included facility mileage,

Table 4. HPMS data items (*67*).

No.	Data Item	No.	Data Item
1	Year of Data	49	Standard Sample Expansion Factor
2	State Code	50	Surface/Pavement Type
3	Reporting Units – Metric or English	51	Structural Number or Thickness
4	County Code	52	General Climate Zone
5	Section Identification	53	Year of Surface Improvement
6	Is Standard Sample	54	Lane Width
7	Is Donut Sample	55	Access Control
8	State Control Field	56	Median Type
9	Is Section Grouped?	57	Median Width
10	Linear Referencing System (LRS) Identification	58	Shoulder Type
11	LRS Beginning Point	59	Shoulder Width – Right
12	LRS Ending Point	60	Shoulder Width – Left
13	Rural/Urban Designation	61	Peak Parking
14	Urbanized Area Sampling Technique	62	Widening Feasibility
15	Urbanized Area Code	63-68	Curves by Class
16	National Ambient Air Quality Standards (NAAQS) Nonattainment Area Code	69	Horizontal Alignment Adequacy
17	Functional System Code	70	Type of Terrain
18	Generated Functional System Code	71	Vertical Alignment Adequacy
19	National Highway System	72-77	Grades by Class
20	Planned Unbuilt Facility	78	Percent Passing Sight Distance
21	Official Interstate Route Number	79	Weighted Design Speed
22	Route Signing	80	Speed Limit
23	Route Signing Qualifier	81	Percent Peak Single Unit Trucks
24	Signed Route Number	82	Percent Average Daily Single Unit Trucks
25	Governmental Ownership	83	Percent Peak Combination Trucks
26	Special Systems	84	Percent Average Daily Combination Trucks
27	Type of Facility	85	K-Factor
28	Designated Truck Route	86	Directional Factor
29	Toll	87	Number of Peak Lanes
30	Section Length	88	Left Turning Lanes/Bays
31	Donut Area Sample Annual Average Daily Traffic (AADT) Volume Group Identifier	89	Right Turning Lanes/Bays
32	Standard Sample AADT Volume Group Identifier	90	Prevailing Type of Signalization
33	AADT	91	Typical Peak Percent Green Time
34	Number of Through Lanes	92	Number At-Grade Intersections – Signals
35	Measured Pavement Roughness	93	Number At-Grade Intersections – Stop Signs
36	Present Serviceability Rating	94	Number At-Grade Intersections – Other or No Controls
37	High Occupancy Vehicle (HOV) Operations	95	Peak Capacity
38-46	Highway Surveillance Systems	96	Volume/Service Flow Ratio
47	Sample Identifier	97	Future AADT
48	Donut Area Sample Expansion Factor	98	Year of Future AADT

travel, and accident statistics. After the merge, a single system evolved to include the "universe" data attributes in MFRS and the area-wide data attributes in the original HPMS.

- In 1988, HPMS was enhanced to include pavement data items, including International Roughness Index (IRI) measurements.
- In 1993, HPMS underwent several modifications to address changes in FHWA analysis and simulation models, 1990 census effects, ISTEA, the Clean Air Act Amendments of 1990, and EPA requirements for vehicle miles traveled (VMT) data in air quality non-attainment areas. The 1993

revision added several "universe" data items for the National Highway System and other principal arterial highways. The amount of sample traffic data for urbanized air quality non-attainment areas increased. Truck data requirements also increased. At the same time, the revision deleted several pavement data items and sample data items for rural minor collectors.

- In 1999, FHWA conducted a major HPMS reassessment (*73*). The reassessment, which began in 1996, removed 15 data items and changed 21 others to eliminate duplication with NHTSA's Fatality Analysis Reporting System. The reassessment reduced the HPMS sample size by 35 percent and the number of records by two-thirds through grouping.

- In 2005, FHWA started another HPMS reassessment. This reassessment included a number of cross-cutting topics, such as process improvements, data quality, data models, sampling, boundaries, and functional classifications (68). Documentation related to the reassessment effort includes a final report (68), data specifications (74), and a field manual (75). Some of the changes in HPMS include the addition of motorcycle travel data, ramps, pavement metadata, traffic metadata, and ownership codes. Other data changes include a reduction in the number of data elements that states need to collect (from 87 to 68). Another major change in the recent HPMS reassessment is an updated data model for HPMS data, which includes several subject areas (called catalogs), including shapes, summaries, references, metadata, sections, and estimates. FHWA is currently conducting training and technical support activities, and expects 2009 data submissions using the updated HPMS data model in 2010.

Although state DOTs recognize that correct and complete HPMS data influence state apportionments of federal funds, a significant challenge for state DOTs is the availability of funds to support the collection and reporting of HPMS data. Unlike other federal data collection programs, there are no dedicated (i.e., earmarked) funds to support this effort (68). Within FHWA, the primary source of funding for HPMS is discretionary research funds. States often use state planning and research funds to collect HPMS data. HPMS data collection and processing can be expensive. The 1999 HPMS reassessment estimated the cost of collecting HPMS data at about $15 million per year nationwide (or about $300,000 per year per state on average) (73). Collecting sample data is the most expensive component, representing 63 percent of the data collection costs. Data collection costs influence the number of collected data items, transportation system scope, and data quality requirements.

FHWA is responsible for maintaining HPMS data provided by state DOTs. In turn, state DOTs are responsible for the accuracy and timely collection and reporting of HPMS data (67). Although FHWA does not specify data collection techniques or perform detailed quality control analyses on the data, FHWA provides assistance with the following:

- Quality assurance using tools as the TranStats HPMS Map Viewer and a 5-year trend table;
- A restricted server side application, which may be accessed on the Internet, that states must use to submit HPMS data (prior versions of this tool were stand-alone versions);
- Annual reviews of state DOT data, including reviews of high-risk items such as traffic data and inventory data, as well as certifying that the state's public road mileage data,

VMT data, and lane-mile data are valid and suitable for use in apportionment of federal-aid highway funds; and

- Coordination between FHWA and state DOTs on HPMS improvements.

HPMS sample data are stratified by state, type of area, highway functional system, and AADT group. The sample size is estimated based on AADT within each stratum, which is the most variable data item. Although the sampling error can be estimated directly based on the sample design for each stratum, this exercise has not been repeated since the 1980s because of the amount of work involved (76).

The impact of non-sampling errors in HPMS is significant. For example, there are guidelines on how to measure data elements such as AADT, but many states use their own procedures. Some data elements may be collected by agencies other than the state DOTs (e.g., MPOs and cities) following different procedures, frequently as an alternative to purchasing commercial datasets. Some data items may be difficult and/or costly to collect, and, as a result, are reported using estimates.

Likewise, states use different methodologies to measure pavement condition ratings. The frequency of pavement inspections also varies from state to state (77). For example, pavement inspections for state systems vary from every year to every other year. However, inspections for non-state systems can vary from every year, to every other year, to every sixth year. The time lag from the date of the pavement inspection to the date when HPMS data are available can be several years.

Lessons Learned

Lessons learned in connection with the development, evolution, and maintenance of HPMS follow:

- **Involve stakeholders through a variety of mechanisms and technologies.** Both the 1999 and the 2010 HPMS reassessments included extensive outreach, ongoing communication, and coordination with stakeholders through various approaches. One of these approaches was through steering committees comprised of federal, state, and local officials, which met several times to identify critical issues and provide oversight. Another approach was to prepare issue papers covering relevant technical issues and data areas, such as sampling, boundaries and functional classification, safety, pavements, interchanges, freight, capacity, data quality, process improvement, and data models.

    Other methods to involve stakeholders included presentations before committees, such as TRB data committees, the AASHTO Standing Committee on Planning (SCOP), the Association of Metropolitan Planning Organizations (AMPO), and Washington-based organizations involved in transportation, as well as regional workshops and follow-up surveys. There were also meetings and interviews with federal employees who were HPMS "customers" or were involved in federal data and policy analysis activities. Communication technology made the process easier, particularly in the case of the 2010 HPMS reassessment, which made extensive use of webinars, posting issue papers online, and receiving comments by e-mail.

- **Evaluate user and data needs carefully to avoid scope creep.** Although systems need to be flexible and adaptable, frequent and uncontrolled changes in scope (i.e., scope creep) can result in cost overruns, missed deadlines, and loss of original goals. In 1999, there were some questions as to the need for HPMS (*68*). To reduce state DOT HPMS data collection costs, the 1999 HPMS reassessment reviewed the need and requirements for each data item in detail (*73*). Implementing the results of this review was estimated to result in potential annual cost savings of $3 million to $5 million nationwide. The data item review included the following items:
  - Determine if the data were needed to meet a legislative requirement, were used in analysis and policy decision activities, were included in state or local highway databases, were quantitative (versus subjective), could be collected with consistency, or could be simulated or estimated (as opposed to collected);
  - Evaluate data aggregation levels;
  - Evaluate if the data should be collected for all sections or for a sample of sections;
  - Evaluate whether the data collected met HPMS mission and objectives and constituted an improvement over the current system, including an evaluation of implementation costs versus savings, potential impacts when data elements are analyzed as a group, and process and timing requirements; and
  - Gather public input and obtain final FHWA internal review and adoption.

  In addition to identifying core data items and processes to reduce the data collection burden on state DOTs, the 1999 reassessment identified a number of needed system enhancements, including the following:
  - Improve the quality of HPMS data;
  - Increase the use of new technology to collect HPMS data;
  - Improve training to states and other data collection agencies;
  - Develop better integration, linkages, and coordination among state, regional, and local databases;
  - Allow access to raw or disaggregated HPMS data for local use;
  - Design HPMS to be statistically significant at the local level; and
  - Include additional pavement condition data.
- **Phase implementation of system changes.** Coordinating the implementation of HPMS changes with the annual

timing of ongoing data collection programs is critical. For the 2010 HPMS reassessment, FHWA decided to implement HPMS in four phases (early, immediate, phased, and late) to focus first on critical data collection and reporting requirements while allowing for future anticipated changes (e.g., changes to boundaries and functional classes following the decennial census).

National Income and Product Accounts

Purpose and Content

BEA's economic accounts are records of economic activity in the United States that provide information about the structure and performance of the U.S. economy (*78–80*). BEA uses a variety of economic accounts, including national economic accounts, regional economic accounts, international economic accounts, and industry economic accounts. There are three main national economic accounts:

- **National Income and Product Accounts.** The NIPAs document the value and composition of national output and the distributions of incomes generated in the production of that output. These accounts help to provide measures of the output of the economy, the sources and uses of national income, and the sources of savings. A key summary measure is the GDP. Other summary measures track personal income, corporate profits, government spending, national production, distribution, consumption, investment, and savings.
- **Industry Input-Output (I-O) accounts.** These accounts document the flow and value of goods and services by industry, the commodity composition of national output, and GDP by industry.
- **Federal Reserve Board flow of funds accounts.** These accounts document the acquisition and value of financial assets, nonfinancial assets, and liabilities, as well as the sources of the funds used to acquire those assets and liabilities.

This review focuses on the NIPAs. The NIPA framework consists of seven summary accounts that contain data aggregated from approximately 300 supporting NIPA tables that contain production and expenditure data by sector, product, function, and investment source. The seven summary accounts are as follows:

1. Domestic income and product account,
2. Private enterprise income account,
3. Personal income and outlay account,
4. Government receipts and expenditures account,
5. Foreign transactions current account,

6. Domestic capital account, and
7. Foreign transactions capital account.

The supporting tables are available on the BEA Website and also can be downloaded in .xls or .csv formats (81). The BEA Web interface enables users to access data annually or quarterly within a specified year range.

Examples of NIPA uses include the following (80):

- Macroeconomic analysis and forecasting,
- U.S. economic measurement,
- Economic policymaking and evaluation,
- Federal budget and tax projection preparation,
- International economy comparison,
- Evaluation of interrelationships between different economic sectors,
- Financial and investment planning by businesses and individuals, and
- Development of other economic accounts.

BEA uses a number of satellite accounts that provide more detail than the NIPAs and facilitate the analysis of specific aspects of the economy. The transportation satellite accounts (TSAs), which were jointly developed by BTS and BEA, focus on transportation services and the contribution of these services to the U.S. economy (82). These accounts make a distinction between hired transportation services and transportation services that businesses provide for their own use, identify industries that account for most transportation activities or are the largest users of transportation services, estimate the impact of transportation in the production costs of these industries, and estimate relative expenditures in transportation infrastructure and equipment by government and businesses.

Development, Challenges, Strategies, and Adaptability

The origin of the NIPAs can be traced back to the 1930s with the publication of the first estimates of national income, which were needed to measure the effectiveness of the strategies implemented to combat the Great Depression (83). In 1942, annual estimates of gross national product (GNP) were introduced and estimates were developed to detail how income was generated, received, and spent by various sectors of the economy. In 1947, the national income and product estimates were integrated into a complete, consistent accounting system with 48 tables. Since then, there have been annual revisions and several comprehensive revisions. Table 5 summarizes major milestones associated with the development and evolution of the NIPAs (83, 84).

Table 5. Major milestones in the development of the NIPAs.

Year	Major Milestones/Revisions
1934	First publication of national income estimates
1942	Annual GNP estimates introduced to complement the estimates of national income
1947	National income and product statistics presented as part of a complete, consistent accounting system
1954	Estimates of real GNP and implicit price deflators added to the NIPA tables
1958	Five summary accounts adopted Quarterly estimates of real GNP, regional estimates, and estimates of the net stock of fixed assets in manufacturing introduced Government-sector tables and foreign-transactions tables modified
1965	Components of GNP benchmarked for the first time in the 1958 I-O table
1976	Estimates of consumption of fixed capital (CFC) shifted to a current-cost basis
1985	Quality-adjusted price indexes for computers and peripheral equipment introduced
1991	National production measure changed from GNP to GDP
1993	NIPA improvements started following the System of National Accounts 1993 framework
1996	Methods for estimating changes in real GDP and for CFC calculation improved Government expenditures for equipment and structures recognized as fixed investment
1999	Several key definitions improved New method introduced for calculating real value of non-priced bank services Consumer price indexes revised back to 1978
2003	More advanced measures of insurance services and banking services adopted New treatment of government activity adopted National income definition expanded to follow international guidelines New tables including two new summary accounts added
2009	New treatments of disasters and insurance services provided by government enterprises introduced Transactions between the federal government and U.S. territories and commonwealths reclassified New classification system for personal consumption expenditures added 2002 benchmark I-O accounts incorporated Statistical measure for estimating personal consumption expenditures, wages and salaries, and proprietors' income improved

Comprehensive revisions have normally taken place at 5-year intervals that correspond with the integration of updated statistics from BEA's benchmark I-O accounts (85). The comprehensive revisions typically introduce major improvements to definitions and classifications, statistical methods, and/or presentations of NIPA tables. Annual revisions complement the comprehensive revisions. The annual revisions generally take place each summer and cover the last 3 years. In 2010, BEA will start using "flexible" annual revisions that will retain the features of the current annual revisions while allowing for improvements normally associated with the major revisions (85).

Data for the economic accounts come from a variety of sources, including the U.S. Census Bureau, BEA, USDA, BLS, the U.S. Treasury Department, the Internal Revenue Service (IRS), and OMB. Close cooperation from these agencies is critical for the production of the NIPAs. BEA complements government-produced or -maintained data with data from trade associations, businesses, international organizations, and other sources. After collecting the data, BEA processes the data and produces NIPA estimates using a combination of statistical methods.

BEA uses the following criteria and methodologies to maintain the usefulness and effectiveness of the NIPA estimates (80):

- **Accuracy.** Accuracy refers to how close the estimates measure the concepts they are designed to measure. In order to keep pace with innovations in the economy, BEA periodically reviews and updates procedures and data to make sure they provide complete, consistent estimates.
- **Reliability.** Reliability refers to the size and frequency of NIPA estimate revisions. BEA's objective is to develop initial estimates that provide reliable indicators of economic growth characteristics and where the economy is in relation to the business cycle.
- **Relevance.** Relevance refers to the length of time before estimates become available and the ability of the accounts to provide estimates that help answer relevant questions. To address the first issue, BEA has developed a release cycle for the estimates, which addresses timeliness and accuracy tradeoffs. To address the second issue, BEA has periodically incorporated improvements to the NIPAs and the other economic accounts to ensure the estimates reflect current conditions and changes in analytical and statistical practice.
- **Integrity.** Integrity refers to the independence and objectiveness of the estimates. To ensure integrity, BEA strives to develop objective, timely estimates and make its processes open and transparent.

In addition, BEA devotes considerable time and effort to ensure the security of the data before releasing any data to the public (86). For example, physical and computer access to sensitive information is restricted, estimates are accessible only to authorized individuals, employees are prevented from pre-releasing information, and releases follow a predetermined schedule.

BEA relies on its own research and development workforce for the preparation of the NIPAs and other economic accounts (80). BEA also relies on scholars and experts from various sources to improve definitions, presentations, and relevant statistical methods.

Lessons Learned

Lessons learned in connection with the development, evolution, and maintenance of the NIPAs follow:

- **Emphasize data quality, reliability, and integrity.** A critical requirement for BEA has been to ensure that calculations and estimates be accurate, reliable, and relevant. Integrity in the form of objective, timely estimates and open, transparent processes are also key requirements. Meeting these requirements is critical to ensure the public's trust in processes and data.
- **Schedule major and regular revisions effectively.** The NIPA revision process consists of annual revisions and comprehensive revisions. The comprehensive revisions enable not just the revision of estimates, but also a review of NIPA definitions, statistical methods, and presentations of NIPA tables. Comprehensive revisions take place at regular intervals (every 5 years) that correspond with the integration of updated statistics from BEA's benchmark I-O accounts. This regularity provides a sense of continuity and ensures the feasibility and relevance of the NIPA process.

National ITS Architecture

Purpose and Content

The National ITS Architecture is a collection of tools that describe functions, entities or subsystems where these functions reside, and data flows that connect functions and subsystems in connection with the implementation of systems that use computing, sensing, and communication technologies in transportation operations (87). The National ITS Architecture has been used for many implementations around the country, including traffic management centers (TMCs), traffic signal systems, and tolling operations.

The National ITS Architecture includes user services, a logical architecture, a physical architecture, and standards, as summarized below.

- **User services.** User services represent what a system would do from the perspective of the user. A user might be the public or a system operator. Currently, there are 33 user services grouped into eight categories (called bundles).

- **Logical architecture.** The logical architecture defines processes, data flows among processes, terminators (i.e., entry and exit points such as sensors, computers, and human operators), and data stores required to satisfy the functional requirements of the 33 user services (*88*). The logical architecture is presented to readers using nested data flow diagrams (DFDs) that provide graphical representations of processes, data flows, terminators, and data stores at various disaggregation levels.

At the highest level is a DFD called Manage ITS that has nine first-level processes, all of which are DFDs. In turn, each of these processes has subordinate processes, some of which are DFDs. Version 6.0 of the National ITS Architecture includes 3,475 logical data flows, of which 344 data flows have as a source node one of the Manage Commercial Vehicles processes or subprocesses. Freight-related data elements typically cover vehicles and their interaction with the road environment. However, some elements address cargo data needs.

- **Physical architecture.** The physical architecture provides a representation (although not a detailed design) of how an integrated system would provide the functionality defined by the user services and the logical architecture. This goal is achieved by defining subsystems based on functional similarity of process specifications and physical locations of functions within the transportation system. As Figure 6 shows, there are four general categories of subsystems: Centers, Field, Travelers, and Vehicles. In general, the physical architecture handles subsystems, architectural flows (that connect subsystems and terminators), and equipment packages (that break up subsystems into deployment-sized pieces).

The physical architecture also handles market packages, which represent slices of the physical architecture that address specific services. In general, a market package includes several different subsystems, equipment packages, terminators, and architectural flows that provide the desired service. The physical architecture includes 13 market packages related to commercial vehicle operation (CVO).

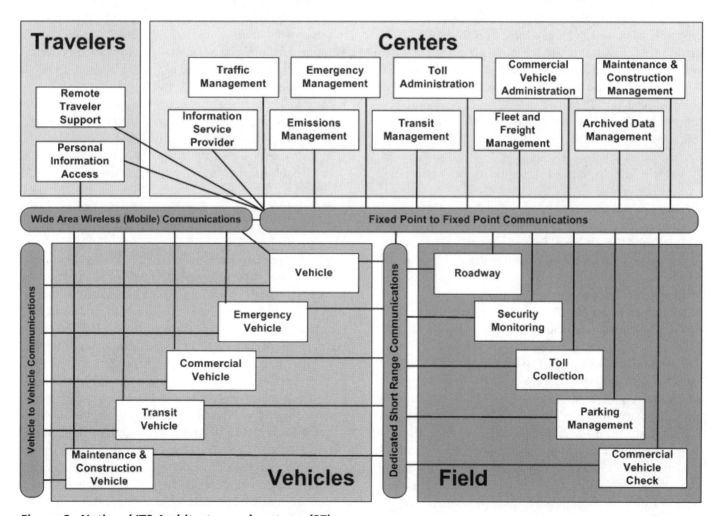

Figure 6. National ITS Architecture subsystems (87).

38

- **Standards.** There are 96 ITS standards in the RITA ITS standard database (without including withdrawn or suspended standards): 2 standards under development, 2 standards in ballot, 4 approved standards, and 88 published standards (*89*). The standards include document types such as guides, data dictionaries, message sets, and protocols.

Although the National ITS Architecture is generic, it can be tailored to meet unique local or regional transportation needs. In the architecture, functions, subsystems, and data flows have precise definitions and associated data elements, which facilitates data exchange within and among jurisdictions at several levels. Readers should note that the National ITS Architecture is not a system architecture in that it does not prescribe specific hardware or software configurations and interfaces, leaving that responsibility to individual agencies that implement the systems.

Development, Challenges, Strategies, and Adaptability

The U.S.DOT manages the implementation of the National ITS Architecture through a program governed by a board of directors called the ITS Management Council (*90*). In 2006, the RITA Administrator became the Chair of the ITS Management Council and, in this capacity, has overall responsibility for the strategic direction and oversight of the ITS Program. In 2004, the ITS Management Council reorganized the functions of the ITS Program to focus on the following nine initiatives:

1. Vehicle Infrastructure Integration (recently renamed IntelliDrive^SM),
2. Next Generation 9-1-1,
3. Cooperative Intersection Collision Avoidance Systems,
4. Integrated Vehicle Based Safety Systems,
5. Integrated Corridor Management Systems,
6. Clarus,
7. Emergency Transportation Operations,
8. Mobility Services for All Americans, and
9. Electronic Freight Management.

The national ITS Program started with the Intelligent Vehicle/Highway Systems (IVHS) initiative in the late 1980s, which focused on the development and implementation of advanced technologies to improve mobility, enhance safety, and maximize the use of existing facilities, at a time when the bulk of the Interstate highway construction program was ending (*91, 92*). IVHS was an effort to better integrate a host of related technologies such as advanced traffic management systems (ATMS), advanced traveler information systems (ATIS), advanced vehicle control systems (AVCS), and CVO.

During the late 1980s and early 1990s, U.S. investments in IVHS were relatively minor, although growing. For example, U.S.DOT's research expenditures in IVHS were $2.3 million in fiscal year 1990 but grew to about $20 million in fiscal year 1991 (*93*). A number of organizations recognized the increasing role of advanced technology in transportation and called for actions such as increasing the level of funding for research and demonstration programs, developing organizational arrangements involving public and private sectors, and including IVHS in federal legislation. Impetus for work in this area in the United States was also the awareness of major IVHS investments in Europe and Japan and the concern that the United States might lose its competitive advantage and become dependent on foreign developments.

Two significant efforts that shaped the future of IVHS were Mobility 2000 (*91, 92*) and TRB *Special Report 232* (*94*). Mobility 2000, an informal group of representatives of universities, industry, and federal, state, and local governments, conducted workshops in 1989 and 1990 that

- Produced key recommendations (including developing an organizational structure to develop policy and legislative recommendations related to IVHS);
- Estimated the investment needs in IVHS by different sectors (including federal, local, and private) to be around $34 billion through year 2010; and
- Identified institutional needs, including developing a framework to facilitate the development of standards for interfaces and communications, noting that efforts should be made to coordinate ATMS, ATIS, AVCS, and CVO elements in a flexible manner to accommodate changes.

Mobility 2000 led to the formation of IVHS America in 1990 (later to become ITS America) as a private, non-profit membership organization with a mission to advise the U.S.DOT and serve as the primary representative of the IVHS community.

TRB *Special Report 232* was the result of an effort by the U.S.DOT, NCHRP, TRB, and private industry from 1988 to 1991 to document a vision for IVHS and formulate specific recommendations for implementing IVHS (*94*). The report evaluated the Mobility 2000 recommendations and identified key IVHS components and issues, including the following:

- It formalized the concept of an IVHS system architecture as the framework within which individual systems and components would operate and relate to each other. The architecture would be a standards-based open system architecture to ensure component interoperability and interchangeability. The report also identified a requirement for the architecture to be flexible to accommodate changes in requirements and technology.

- It recognized the need to identify human-machine interfaces, specifically, the information processing demands that IVHS would impose on human operators and users.
- It highlighted the need to use a systems engineering approach for developing the architecture as well as the need to evaluate alternative architecture approaches.
- It recommended the U.S.DOT (in a leadership role) and IVHS America (in an advisory role) work together to implement the IVHS program.

TRB *Special Report 232* also included a summary of the development of other similar architectures, specifically, those associated with the Aeronautical Telecommunications Network (ATN), the Advanced Train Control Systems (ATCS) Project, and the European Dedicated Road Infrastructure for Vehicle Safety (DRIVE) Program.

In 1991, ISTEA (*69*) resulted in significant increases in IVHS investment levels (*95*). As a reference, Table 6 provides a summary of critical pieces of federal legislation related to IVHS and ITS since 1991, along with the corresponding allocation of federal funds.

In 1991, the U.S. General Accounting Office (GAO) reviewed 38 major studies conducted in the 1980s and concluded that IVHS was seen as promising, although the empirical evidence for judging its benefits was still limited (*93*). In addition to the need for a more detailed analysis of anticipated benefits and costs, the 1991 GAO report identified three types of barriers (cost barriers, institutional barriers, and technological barriers) that could affect the overall success of IVHS. In particular were the following:

- The report recommended finding a proper mix of burden sharing between private and government sectors to absorb the costs of developing and operating IVHS, noting that an inappropriate distribution of costs could prevent full realization of IVHS potential.
- The report highlighted the requirement for various stakeholders to work together to ensure the success of IVHS and the need to focus on setting standards (which would also require cooperation and coordination among participants).

The ISTEA mandate called for a three-pronged effort, including basic research and development, operational tests, and deployment support activities. Nonetheless, a 1994 GAO report on traffic control signal systems found that federal protocols to review state and local governments' operations plans for signal systems were inconsistent and that technical expertise deficiencies of FHWA staff, which FHWA had identified in 1990, had not improved significantly (*95*).

During the early 1990s, the U.S.DOT developed strategic and program plans for implementing IVHS. At that time, FHWA had primary responsibility for the program, although the FTA and NHTSA also had active roles in funding and managing IVHS projects. State and local governments, private industry, and the research community were active participants in shaping the program and conducting research and operational tests. Significant input also was available through IVHS America.

A critical initiative in the early 1990s was the development of a national architecture and standards for IVHS. The main motivation for this development was the recognition that the absence of common IVHS architecture and standards in Europe was having a negative impact on the European Community's goal of a seamless IVHS environment across national boundaries, delaying the development of a common market for European IVHS products. The vision for the national IVHS architecture in the United States was that it would define a general framework within which IVHS system components would work, while standards would specify the technical requirements of individual IVHS applications. Developing a national IVHS architecture would ensure compatibility among different IVHS hardware and software technologies and accelerate the implementation of IVHS by reducing the risks to private- and public-sector stakeholders. Without the assurance of compatibility, stakeholders would be reluctant to invest in IVHS infrastructure.

Table 6. Important pieces of federal legislation related to IVHS and ITS.

Legislation	Comment/Allocation of Funds*
ISTEA (ITS Program: 1992–1997)	$659 million for research and testing $564 million for deployment Total: $1.22 billion
National Highway System Designation Act	Replaced IVHS with ITS.
TEA-21 (ITS Program: 1998–2005), including a 2-year extension	$823 million for research and testing $923 million for deployment Total: $1.75 billion
SAFETEA-LU (ITS Program: 2006–2009)	$440 million for research and testing Deployment was discontinued Total: $440 million

* Fund allocation information provided by the U.S.DOT.

To develop a common national IVHS architecture, the U.S.DOT instituted an IVHS architecture development program and contracted several key aspects of this development, including the following (*96*):

- **System architecture development.** The first phase involved four contractors (Hughes Aircraft, Loral, Rockwell International, and Westinghouse) to develop candidate IVHS architectures (*97*). The second phase involved a consortium between Loral and Rockwell International to develop the most promising architecture concepts from the first phase into a single architecture. This architecture was completed in July 1996.
- **System architecture manager.** The purpose of this contract (awarded to NASA's Jet Propulsion Laboratory) was to work closely with the architecture development teams, providing technical review and evaluation of the candidate architectures.
- **System architecture consensus building.** The purpose of this contract was to develop an outreach program, including regional briefings on the progress of the IVHS architecture definition effort.
- **Commercial vehicle operations institutional issues.** The purpose of these studies was to evaluate institutional issues that would impede the achievement of national commercial vehicle operations goals.

The U.S.DOT has continued to support the architecture through deployment and maintenance contracts. According to information provided by the U.S.DOT, the total federal investment on the architecture program has been $65 million so far.

During the mid 1990s, ITS—federal legislation replaced IVHS references with ITS in 1995—grew rapidly, from a few projects in 1992 to 268 projects in 1995. Appropriations also grew to more than $800 million (*98, 99*). By the end of 1996, the total federal funding committed to ITS since 1991 had grown to $1.2 billion.

In the mid 1990s, FHWA changed the focus of the ITS Program from research and operational tests to deployment and training. FHWA viewed outreach and training as critical because of the realization (backed by several studies) that many local officials did not have the technical skills needed to operate and maintain ITS infrastructure investments (*100*). One of the reasons for this shortage was that most transportation agencies had staff with a background in civil engineering, not electrical engineering or systems integration. Lack of ITS awareness also was common among agency managers and decisionmakers. These limitations were barriers to successful ITS deployment. Additional barriers were the lack of economic models that local transportation officials could use to determine the costs and benefits of ITS implementations, making it difficult to justify expenditures on ITS-related projects (*100*) and a lack of funds at the local level to support these projects in light of other transportation priorities (*101*).

In 1998, TEA-21 consolidated this trend by launching a transition to more integrated ITS application deployments. In the process, it consolidated eight ITS program areas into two subprograms: infrastructure (metropolitan infrastructure, rural infrastructure, and commercial vehicle infrastructure) and intelligent vehicle initiatives (including Commercial Vehicle Information Systems and Networks [CVISN]) (*102*). It also recognized the need to accelerate the development of standards and the identification of critical standards to ensure national interoperability. Specific strategies the U.S.DOT pursued at that time to address challenges affecting ITS deployments included the following:

- Accelerate the development of standards,
- Provide professional capacity training,
- Conduct ITS infrastructure and vehicle research,
- Provide ITS deployment assistance,
- Conduct workshops to encourage consistency with the National ITS Architecture and standards,
- Showcase the benefits of integrated deployments, and
- Evaluate the ITS program.

In 2001, the U.S.DOT finalized a rule (23 CFR 940.9) requiring ITS projects to conform to a regional architecture (*103*). The purpose of the rule was to ensure compliance with national standards in a regional, integrated way. Regions and states were required to complete their regional ITS architectures by April 2005 (if they had ITS implementations in 2001) or within 4 years of the first ITS project advancing to final design (if the region or state did not have an ITS implementation in 2001).

In 2005, SAFETEA-LU ended the ITS deployment program, although it continued to support ITS research and operational testing at $110 million each year through fiscal year 2009. (Note: ITS projects are still eligible for regular federal-aid highway funding.) Relevant provisions in SAFETEA-LU related to ITS in connection with this research included the following:

- It required states and regions developing or updating their regional ITS architectures to address real-time highway and transit information needs, and the systems needed to meet those needs. The regional ITS architectures also had to incorporate data exchange formats to ensure the data from highway and transit monitoring systems could be made available to state and local governments as well as to the traveling public.

- It required the designation of a panel of experts to recommend ways to expedite and streamline the process of developing standards and protocols.

In 2005, GAO (which by then had been renamed as the U.S. Government Accountability Office) reviewed a variety of reports that documented ITS deployments around the country and interviewed officials from several agencies at the federal, state, and local level (*104*). The report concluded that, although ITS technologies could be beneficial to help relieve congestion, the original goal to deploy ITS systems to relieve congestion had not been met. The report highlighted that measures the U.S.DOT had in place to determine deployment levels (e.g., whether a metropolitan area had transportation management centers) were inadequate and did not take into consideration other factors such as operational requirements (e.g., number of hours a center had to operate each day). The report also identified a number of barriers to ITS deployment, including the following:

- At the state or local levels, viewing options such as adding a new highway lane more favorably than ITS when deciding how to spend transportation funds;
- Lack of funding for both ITS installations and operations and lack of awareness that federal funds also can be used for operational costs;
- Lack of technical expertise at the local and state level; and
- Lack of technical standards, slow pace in standard development, or standards that do not keep pace with technological advances.

According to information provided by the U.S.DOT, the total federal investment on the development of standards has been $109.3 million so far ($20 million under ISTEA, $68 million under TEA-21, and $21.3 million under SAFETEA-LU). As previously mentioned, there are 96 ITS standards in the RITA ITS standard database (without including withdrawn or suspended standards) (*89*). Nonetheless, the lack of standards and the slow pace in standard development are frequently cited as important factors that explain ITS deployments delays. The standards development process can be a lengthy process. In some cases, technological innovations evolve faster than standards.

The RITA administrator became the chair of the ITS Management Council in 2006 (*90*). The ITS Management Council develops and directs federal ITS policy and ensures the effectiveness of the ITS Program. Members of the council include the following:

- Under secretary of transportation for policy,
- Assistant secretary for transportation policy and intermodalism,

- U.S.DOT's chief information officer,
- FHWA administrator,
- FMCSA administrator,
- FTA administrator,
- NHTSA administrator,
- RITA administrator (chair),
- FRA administrator, and
- Maritime Administration (MARAD) administrator.

The ITS Strategic Planning Group advises the ITS Management Council. The group, which is chaired by the ITS program manager, includes members at the associate administrator and office director level.

The ITS program manager leads the ITS Joint Program Office (JPO), which includes program managers and coordinators of the U.S.DOT's multimodal ITS initiatives. The program includes staff support for functions such as Website development and maintenance, outreach, program evaluation, training, architecture, and standards. The ITS Joint Program Office is administratively located in FHWA under the policy direction of RITA.

Archived ITS Data

The national ITS Program evolved primarily to assist real-time and near-real-time transportation operations needs. Although placeholders for transportation planning needs were included in the National ITS Architecture from the beginning, and there were examples of traffic sensor data archival efforts going back to the 1970s, the process to develop an archived data user service (ADUS) only started in 1997 after the first release of the National ITS Architecture (*105*). ADUS was added as a user service in Version 3 of the architecture in 1999.

As with other user services, which represent what a system would do from the perspective of the user, ADUS provides tools and describes processes related to ITS data archiving. Although all ITS deployments use and/or produce data, ADUS is not mandatory. However, having ADUS in the architecture facilitates the inclusion of ITS data archival functions in ITS deployments.

Over the last 10 years, the focus on ADUS development has been the development of standards. Currently, there are three ITS standards for archived ITS data. The first standard, published in 2003, provides guidance for archiving and retrieving ITS data. The second standard, published in 2006, contains a metadata standard for ITS data. The foundation for this standard was the FGDC metadata standard (*106*). The third standard, published in 2008, contains a detailed data dictionary for archived ITS data. Unfortunately, additional work on archived ITS data standards stopped due to lack of funding. This funding was used to pay a consultant to do the technical

42

work and support travel of public-sector officials to attend standards development meetings.

Lessons Learned

Lessons learned in connection with the development, evolution, and maintenance of the National ITS Architecture (and associated standards) follows:

- **Involve stakeholders early and often.** It was critical to involve various stakeholders (federal, state, and local governments, as well as private industry) early to develop a vision for a national ITS Program. These stakeholders also had a clear picture of what a national ITS architecture (and related standards) should focus on and accomplish. Nonetheless, it took nearly 3 years to develop and document that picture. In addition, although the U.S.DOT has played a critical leadership role in the development and implementation of the national ITS Program, other stakeholders also have played a critical role in shaping that program. For example, ITS America continues to provide an advisory, advocacy role on behalf of some 450 member organizations that include public-sector agencies (including state, county, and local levels) and private-sector agencies. Roughly half of the member organizations in ITS America are public-sector agencies.
- **Develop and compare candidate architecture concepts.** The National ITS Architecture as implemented was the result of a two-phase approach. The first phase involved having competing teams develop candidate architecture concepts. The second phase involved selecting a consortium from the first phase and developing an architecture using the best elements from the first phase.
- **Consider federal legislation to support and develop the program.** The ITS program was a major initiative at a time when the bulk of the Interstate highway construction program was ending. Without the support of federal legislation, the U.S.DOT would not have received the level of funding needed to develop and implement the program, as well as to help maintain national attention on that program. Developing and maintaining the National ITS Architecture and standards also was included in the federal legislation.
- **Develop long-term plans with flexibility in mind.** The national ITS Program has evolved since its inception in the early 1990s. Along the way, changes have been instituted to respond to issues that were not anticipated in the original vision. For example, the requirement to develop regional ITS architectures evolved as a strategy to encourage compliance with national standards in a regional, integrated way. There are also ambitious goals that have not fully materialized yet. For example, when the ITS program started, the goal was to fully deploy ITS systems at all major metropolitan areas in the country. However, partly because of the lack of appropriate measures to determine whether that goal was being attained, the current level of ITS deployment is not what the original visionaries had in mind. Likewise, although it was clear from the beginning that national ITS standards had to be developed to ensure compatibility and interoperability, managers of the ITS Program did not anticipate the slow pace with which ITS standards would be developed.

- **Develop tools to measure benefits and costs early.** For many years, the ITS community did not have access to practical tools to measure the costs and benefits of ITS implementations. To assist in this process, RITA now has on its Website benefit and cost databases (including unit costs) to help planners and engineers determine the technical and economic feasibility of their proposed projects. The need for this type of tools became critical after SAFETEA-LU ended the ITS deployment program and ITS projects had to compete for funding just like any other transportation project. A critical requirement in this process is the development of appropriate performance measures to determine the effectiveness of ITS investments.
- **Develop and implement professional capacity and training programs early.** A factor that hampered acceptance and implementation of ITS deployments was the lack of technical skills in critical areas (e.g., systems integration and electrical engineering) to operate and maintain ITS infrastructure investments. Lack of ITS awareness also was common among agency managers and decisionmakers. These limitations were barriers to successful ITS deployments.
- **Integrate archived data needs into frameworks and architectures early.** The national ITS program evolved primarily to assist real-time and near-real-time transportation operations needs. Although placeholders for transportation planning needs were included in the National ITS Architecture from the beginning, the recognition of the need for an archived data user service did not happen until the National ITS Architecture was already published. The development of ITS archived data standards also has been slow. Although there are now three ADUS-related data standards, there are no documented examples of their use yet.

National Spatial Data Infrastructure

Purpose and Content

NSDI is a dissemination effort to "acquire, process, store, distribute, and improve utilization of geospatial data throughout all levels of government, the private and non-profit sectors, and academia" (*106*). NSDI is managed by FGDC. NSDI goals include (1) reducing duplicative efforts among agencies; (2) improving quality and reducing the costs of geospatial data; (3) making the benefits of geographic data more accessible to the public; and (4) establishing partnerships to increase data availability.

NSDI includes five major components, as follows (*106*):

- **Framework.** The framework is a collaborative approach and effort to facilitate the development of datasets that are critical at the national level. The framework has three parts (sometimes presented as four components: information content, technical context, operational context, and business context [*107*]), as follows:
  - Seven data themes (also called framework data): geodetic control, orthoimagery, elevation and bathymetry, transportation, hydrography, cadastral, and governmental units;
  - Procedures and references for building and using framework data, e.g., spatial data models, permanent feature identification codes, support for multiple resolution levels, and a common coordinate referencing system; and
  - Institutional arrangements and business practices to encourage the maintenance and use of the data, e.g., through open, distributed access to framework data.
- **Metadata.** FGDC is responsible for maintaining a metadata standard for geospatial data called Content Standard for Digital Geospatial Metadata (CSDGM). CSDGM became mandatory for federal agencies in January 1995. Nationwide, state and local agencies are increasingly adopting and using CSDGM, partly because of the availability of user-friendly CSDGM editors such as those included in commonly used GIS applications.
- **Standards.** FGDC maintains a list of FGDC-endorsed standards. The standards, which are sponsored and maintained by different organizations including FGDC, cover areas such as data transfer, data content, and geospatial positional accuracy. The status of a standard throughout its life cycle could be one of several options, including reaffirmed, to be determined, not applicable, requiring changes, or retired. It is not clear to what degree FGDC-endorsed standards are used nationwide, particularly by agencies other than the federal agencies that sponsor and/or have maintenance responsibility for individual standards. In the case of content standards (e.g., cadastral, digital orthoimagery, remote sensing swath data, framework data, and utility facilities—which has been retired), the GIS industry is developing and promoting spatial data models outside the FGDC environment, which, in practice, might render some FGDC content standards irrelevant, particularly for state and local agencies.
- **Clearinghouse Network.** The Clearinghouse Network is a community of distributed data providers that publish information about, and links to, available digital spatial data and services. FGDC coordinates sharing geographic data, maps, and online services through the geodata.gov portal (*108*).

- **Partnerships.** Partnerships include institutional arrangements with federal agencies and other recognized stakeholder groups that share a common interest in critical data themes, standards, metadata, and information sharing. To support this effort, FGDC has developed an interagency organizational structure that includes a steering committee, a coordination group, working groups and subcommittees, and partner organizations. Interaction with other agencies also takes place through a variety of initiatives, including the following:
  - Fifty State Initiative, which focuses on assisting states in developing strategic and business plans to facilitate programs, policies, and technologies to support NSDI;
  - NSDI Cooperative Agreements Program, which focuses on assisting the geospatial data community through funding and other resources in implementing NSDI components; and
  - Geospatial Line of Business (LoB), which is a presidential initiative that focuses on fostering collaboration, reducing redundancies, and improving accountability and transparency across the federal government.

Institutional Arrangements, Challenges, and Strategies

Important milestones in the development and evolution of FGDC and NSDI include the following:

- In 1983, OMB established the Federal Interagency Coordinating Committee on Digital Cartography (FICCDC), from which FGDC evolved (*109*).
- In 1990, OMB revised Circular A-16 to establish FGDC within the Department of the Interior to support the nationwide use, sharing, and distribution of geospatial data (*110*).
- In 1994, Presidential Executive Order 12906 made FGDC responsible for coordinating the development of a national spatial data infrastructure to address redundancy and incompatibility issues related to geospatial information (*110*). The same year, FGDC developed a strategy for NSDI with help from stakeholders (*111*).
- In 1997, FGDC developed an updated strategy for NSDI to continue major components of NSDI and to increase awareness (*112*).
- In 2002, OMB revised Circular A-16 to reflect changes in geographic information management and technology, further describe NSDI components, and assign agency roles and responsibilities for the development of NSDI (*113*).
- In 2003, FGDC started a new initiative, called the NSDI Future Directions Initiative, to develop a geospatial strategy and implementation plan for further developing NSDI (*114*).
- In 2007, the U.S. Geological Survey (USGS) selected a contractor to manage the Geospatial LoB initiative under the coordination of FGDC (*115, 116*).

The 1994, 1997, and 2003 strategic plan documents reflect efforts by FGDC to maintain and continue developing NSDI. Most of the initiatives and programs currently in place at FGDC (see previous section) are the result of those plans. However, the 2004 NSDI Future Directions Initiative report acknowledged a number of issues and needs voiced by stakeholders (*114*), including the following:

- Need for more effective data sharing and coordination within the entire geospatial community,
- Need for a level playing field in the design and implementation of NSDI and a need for FGDC to play a neutral facilitator role,
- Lack of an effectively communicated shared vision,
- Lack of a clear business case for stakeholder participation, and
- Emphasis on isolated geospatial programs at many government agencies.

Other reports have produced similar observations. For example, GAO reports in 2003 and 2004 concluded that the NSDI program was successful in promoting basic concepts, the clearinghouse, and development of several standards, including CSDGM (*110, 117*). The CSDGM standard, in particular, is increasingly used outside federal agencies. However, the reports noted a number of issues, including that developing standards to meet stakeholder needs and achieving stakeholder participation remained a challenging task, and that the FGDC reporting process was not sufficiently developed. More importantly, the GAO reports concluded that the NSDI programs had not resulted in significant reductions in geospatial data redundancy and costs or improvements in geospatial data accuracy. Reasons mentioned include the following:

- Lack of up-to-date strategic plans with specific measures for identifying and reducing redundancies,
- Many federal geospatial datasets not being compliant with FGDC standards or published outside NSDI clearinghouse procedures, and
- Lack of effectiveness in OMB's oversight of federal geospatial activities.

A recent National States Geographic Information Council report concluded that there was a need to refocus national efforts to complete the development of NSDI and to devise appropriate data maintenance methods (*118*). This report produced several recommendations, including the following:

- Formulate an effective national strategy for implementing NSDI across federal, state, and local levels;

- Make federal NSDI funding contingent on compliance with collaboratively established criteria and requirements (i.e., similar to the federal highway funding model); and
- Develop a national strategy to communicate about, and advocate for, NSDI.

Finally, although the level of awareness about NSDI is increasing, many geospatial data stakeholders (particularly outside the federal government) have difficulty understanding NSDI's purpose, its governance structure, or its products. There is plenty of documentation (e.g., reports, brochures, presentations, and papers) about NSDI and FGDC, much of it on the FGDC Website (*106*). However, navigating through this information is difficult because the information is not properly grouped or indexed (e.g., by subject or date of publication) which means it is common to find information without proper thematic or temporal context. An example of this situation is the description of the NSDI framework on the NSDI Website. On some pages, the framework is described as having three parts, but on other pages, it is described as having four components. Without a proper thematic or temporal context, it is difficult to understand which categorization is current or if there is a difference between parts and components. Likewise, the NSDI Website provides various inconsistent definitions even for basic terms such as NSDI, NSDI framework, clearinghouse, and partnerships.

Lessons Learned

Lessons learned in connection with the development, evolution, and maintenance of NSDI follow:

- **Articulate programs well and provide good documentation.** Of the five main NSDI components, the metadata and the clearinghouse components have been considered successful. Nationwide, state and local agencies are increasingly adopting and using the CSDGM metadata standard, partly because of the availability of user-friendly CSDGM editors such as those included in commonly used GIS applications. The acceptance of other NSDI components has been mixed. One of the reasons NSDI has not been more successful is the lack of adequate, consistent, properly indexed information and documentation on the FGDC Website. NSDI is frequently considered an ambiguous concept. As a result, many geospatial data stakeholders do not really understand what NSDI is, its purpose, its governance structure, or even its products.
- **Develop systems that are relevant to stakeholders.** As mentioned, the CSDGM standard has been successful partly because user-friendly CSDGM editors are now included in commonly used GIS applications. Another reason is that CSDGM is more comprehensive than the relatively simple

data dictionaries in use at many agencies nationwide. In other words, migrating to a "better" standard, particularly when the standard implementation is already available on a user-friendly interface, is a logical step. In contrast, migrating to one of the FGDC data content standards might not be desirable, particularly at the state or local level, considering that the GIS industry is developing and promoting spatial data models outside of the FGDC standards environment, which, in practice, might render some FGDC content standards irrelevant.

• **Provide incentives to encourage participation, particularly in the case of state and local entities.** A major impediment cited in relation to the promotion of NSDI nationwide is that states and local jurisdictions do not perceive a benefit in implementing NSDI within their jurisdictions. Lack of funding is another reason frequently cited for the lack of acceptability of NSDI nationwide.

National Transportation Atlas Database

Purpose and Content

NTAD is a product compiled and published by BTS that contains several geographic databases of interest to the transportation community. The transportation atlas is available on digital video disk (DVD) and for download on the BTS Website (*119*). Table 7 shows the list of datasets included in the 2009 version of NTAD. Many of those datasets are relevant to freight planning and operations.

Development, Challenges, Strategies, and Adaptability

ISTEA created BTS with the mission to enhance transportation data collection, analysis, and reporting (*69*). BTS received $90 million to support its activities over a first 6-year period starting in fiscal year 1992. NTAD was one of the early initiatives that BTS undertook (*120*). TEA-21 and SAFETEA-LU reemphasized this commitment by requiring BTS to maintain geographic databases that depict transportation networks; flows of people, goods, vehicles, and craft over the networks; and social, economic, and environmental conditions that affect, or are affected by, the networks (*70, 71*).

BTS released the first NTAD version in 1995, and since then it has continued to publish yearly updates. NTAD was originally published on CDs and then on DVDs. The latest NTAD version is also available online (*119*). The North American Transportation Atlas Database (NORTAD) was a special

Table 7. Datasets included in the 2009 version of NTAD (*119*).

Dataset	Type	Maintained By
111th Congressional Districts Boundaries	Polygon	U.S. Census Bureau
Airport Runways	Polyline	FAA
Airports	Point	FAA
Alternative Fuels	Point	BTS
Amtrak Stations	Point	FRA
Automatic Traffic Recorder Stations	Point	FHWA
Core Based Statistical Areas	Polygon	U.S. Census Bureau
Fixed-Guideway Transit Facilities	Polyline	FTA
Freight Analysis Framework	Polyline	FHWA
Hazardous Material Routes	Polyline	FMCSA
Highway Performance Monitoring System	Polyline	FHWA
Hydrographic Features	Polygon	BTS
Hydrographic Features	Polyline	BTS
Intermodal Terminal Facilities	Point	BTS
Metropolitan Planning Organizations	Polygon	BTS and FHWA
National Bridge Inventory	Point	FHWA
National Highway Planning Network	Point	FHWA
National Highway Planning Network	Polyline	FHWA
National Park System Boundary Dataset	Polygon	National Park Service
National Populated Places	Point	U.S. Census Bureau
Navigable Waterway Network	Polyline	USACE
Non Attainment Areas	Polygon	EPA
Ports	Point	USACE
Railroad Grade Crossings	Point	FRA
Railway Network	Point	FRA
Railway Network	Polyline	FRA
U.S. County Boundaries	Polygon	U.S. Census Bureau
U.S. Military Installations	Polygon	Transportation Engineering Agency
U.S. State Boundaries	Polygon	U.S. Census Bureau
Urbanized Area Boundaries	Polygon	U.S. Census Bureau
Weigh in Motion Stations	Point	FHWA

version in the series, which was published in 1998 in collaboration with Canada and Mexico (*121*). NORTAD contained updated NTAD datasets, border crossings, and datasets depicting Canadian and Mexican transportation infrastructure facilities.

Early NTAD versions followed an American Standard Code for Information Interchange (ASCII) fixed-record-length format that included six distinct record types, as follows (*121*):

1. Link (.lnk file extension);
2. Node (.nod file extension);
3. Point (.pnt file extension);
4. Area (.are file extension);
5. Geography (.geo file extension), which contains shape information for network links and area boundaries; and
6. Attribute (.txx file extensions, e.g., .t01, .t02, and .t03).

Combinations of different record types defined the geometry, topology, and attributes of point, network, and area feature types. BTS made these file formats available to GIS vendors on a temporary basis to facilitate the development of data conversion software tools. In practice, although BTS intended to migrate NTAD to the federal Spatial Data Transfer Standard (SDTS), the ESRI shapefile format became a de facto standard. As a result, since the early 2000s, BTS has published NTAD in this format. It is also worth noting that, although ASCII is still in use, it is quickly being replaced by more modern encoding schemes such as Unicode.

A number of agencies contribute data to NTAD, including BEA, FAA, FHWA, FMCSA, FRA, FTA, the U.S. Census Bureau, and USACE (Table 7). BTS collects data from these participating agencies and then processes and publishes the data within NTAD. Data gathering for NTAD typically starts in November of each year. In general, data creation, maintenance, update, spatial positional accuracy and resolution, and quality control responsibilities remain with the data source agencies. Depending on data format, quality, and completeness, BTS processes data by checking spatial and attribute data characteristics, inserting additional attribute data, and recompiling metadata using the FGDC metadata standard (*122*). Most data processing takes place in an ESRI ArcGIS™ environment.

Lessons Learned

NTAD is a popular data series that remains an important program within BTS and RITA, along with the operation of the FGDC transportation subcommittee (*123*). Budgetary changes have forced the agency to cut back other GIS programs.

Lessons learned in connection with the development, evolution, and maintenance of NTAD follow:

• **Implement interagency data exchange programs with centralized data coordination.** NTAD is a product led by

BTS with data support from a large number of agencies. BTS collects data that those agencies produce and/or maintain, reprocesses the data into a central repository, and then makes the data available to users. This approach takes advantage of existing resources at individual data producers while avoiding data collection and data processing redundancy. BTS's coordination role helps to improve the availability and standardization of critical transportation data and metadata.

• **Develop spatial data programs that use industry standards.** Originally, NTAD used an ASCII fixed-record-length format. However, modern encoding schemes such as Unicode started replacing the ASCII format. In addition, although data conversion tools to enable the conversion of NTAD data to other file formats were available, in practice, the ESRI shapefile format became a de facto standard. As a result, since the early 2000s, BTS has published NTAD in this format.

The advantage of using a de facto standard such as the ESRI shapefile format is that this format is widely used, which facilitates data exchange. The disadvantage is that the shapefile format is an old data format that ESRI no longer maintains (although ESRI GIS software applications provide shapefile format backward compatibility). With the introduction of ArcGIS 8 in 1999, ESRI started using "geodatabases" to store geographic datasets. A geodatabase could be a "personal geodatabase" (in Microsoft® Access® format) or an "ArcSDE™ geodatabase" (with the data stored in a relational database such as Oracle®, Microsoft Structured Query Language [SQL] Server®, IBM® DB2®, or IBM Informix®) (*124*). Recently, ESRI introduced a "file geodatabase" format to address the file size limitations of personal databases (Access files cannot exceed 2 gigabytes in size). Although the use of geodatabases is increasing, at this point it is not clear to what degree federal agencies have started to require their use for data exchange purposes.

General Observations and Lessons Learned

The previous sections included a summary of data sources, systems, and architectures relevant to the freight community. Table 1 provides a listing of the freight data sources, systems, and architectures reviewed, whereas Appendix A of the contractor's final report (available on the project web page) includes a detailed description of each data source, system, or architecture. Although not comprehensive, the review provides a sample of the typical data sources, systems, and architectures that could be included in a national freight data architecture, as well as any potential implementations that could derive from that data architecture.

In general, the material in Appendix A describes the current status and characteristics of the data sources, systems, and architectures reviewed. For the research, it also was important to learn about the process, institutional arrangements, and challenges associated with the development and maintenance of the systems, as well as any strategies that have been deployed to address challenges and other data integration issues, such as data quality, timeliness, and proprietary and privacy concerns. Given the large number of data sources, systems, and architectures uncovered during the literature search (49 according to Table 1), it was not practical to conduct a comprehensive review of historical developments for all of them. However, a few systems and architectures in Table 1 were of interest because of the processes that led to their development (e.g., in the form of issues, motivations, challenges, legislative efforts, and implemented strategies). Lessons learned from those processes can provide valuable information for, and help to minimize the cost of, the development and implementation of a national freight data architecture.

The sample of systems and architectures selected for the detailed historical analysis covered a wide spectrum of topics related to freight transportation and included the following:

- ACE/ITDS,
- Carload Waybill Sample,
- CFS,
- EDI standards,
- FAF,
- HPMS,
- NIPAs,
- National ITS Architecture,
- NSDI, and
- NTAD.

For this sample of systems and architectures, the analysis covered several topics, including the following:

- Purpose and intended benefits;
- Content;
- Institutional arrangements used for developing and maintaining the system or architecture;
- Challenges and issues faced in creating and maintaining the architecture or system;
- Strategies and methods for dealing with data integration issues, such as data quality, timeliness, and proprietary and privacy concerns;
- Adaptability to serve evolving purposes and data sources; and
- Assessment of how well the system or architecture works in the form of lessons learned.

In general, all of the systems and architectures reviewed in this report (including those described in detail in this chapter) relate to processes that affect one or more freight trans-

portation aspects or components (see Chapters 3 and 4 for a more detailed discussion of those aspects and components). From this perspective, all of the systems and architectures in this report should be included at some level in the design of a national freight data architecture if this data architecture is indeed designed to address the needs of both public and private decisionmakers not just at the national level, but also at the state and local levels.

However, identifying which data sources, systems, and architectures to include in a national freight data architecture depends to a large degree on the vision that is laid out for this data architecture. As Chapter 4 describes in more detail, it is possible to outline a number of competing implementation alternatives, some of them more comprehensive and ambitious in scope than others. For example, a freight data architecture that only focuses on commodity flow aspects for planning purposes at the national level requires data sources, systems, and architectures that are both commodity-related and relevant at the national level. By comparison, a freight data architecture that includes commodity, transportation network, vehicle, and safety aspects to address the needs of federal and state governments would require the inclusion of a larger number of finer resolution data sources, systems, and architectures. Likewise, a freight data architecture that includes real-time supply chain data from the private sector would require conducting an analysis of the risks the private sector would assume if it shares sensitive and/or confidential data elements that could undermine its competitive position and decisionmaking process.

Chapter 4 addresses different implementation alternatives that may be possible for a national freight data architecture. However, a summarized list of lessons learned from all of the systems and architectures reviewed is appropriate here because many of the lessons learned are sufficiently generic and, consequently, could be used to guide the development and implementation of any freight data architecture, regardless of implementation level. The summarized list of lessons learned follows:

- Develop systems that are relevant to stakeholders, include adequate stakeholder participation, and provide incentives to encourage participation, particularly in the case of state and local entities (ACE/ITDS, NSDI);
- Clearly define expected outcomes and development and coordination plan (ACE/ITDS);
- Articulate programs well; provide clear, uniform guidance; and provide good documentation (Carload Waybill Sample, NSDI);
- Develop applications that rely on widely used data standards (EDI standards, National ITS Architecture, NSDI);
- Develop and compare candidate architecture concepts (National ITS Architecture);

48

- Consider federal legislation to support and develop the program (National ITS Architecture);
- Develop tools to measure benefits and costs early (National ITS Architecture);
- Integrate archived data needs into frameworks and architectures early and develop data programs that use industry standards (National ITS Architecture, NTAD);
- Implement interagency data exchange programs with centralized data coordination (NTAD);
- Use available data sources and develop long-term plans while keeping systems flexible to respond to changes and new data sources (FAF, HPMS, National ITS Architecture);
- Schedule major and regular revisions effectively while avoiding scope creep (HPMS, NIPAs);
- Develop systems that are consistent with input data limitations (FAF);
- Develop applications with backward compatibility (EDI standards);

- Evaluate data disaggregation level requirements to ensure statistical significance (HPMS);
- Provide adequate resources for data collection, fully understand the implications of small sample sizes, and continue to involve the U.S. Census Bureau for the use of survey instruments (CFS);
- Emphasize data access, quality, reliability, confidentiality, and integrity (Carload Waybill Sample, FAF, NIPAs);
- Participate in the standards development process (EDI standards, National ITS Architecture, NSDI);
- Create crosswalks to ensure compatibility of survey data internally over time and externally across other datasets (CFS);
- Involve stakeholders early and often through a variety of mechanisms and technologies (ACE/ITDS, FAF, HPMS, National ITS Architecture); and
- Develop and implement professional capacity and training programs early (National ITS Architecture).

CHAPTER 3

Surveys, Interviews, and Peer Exchange

Introduction

An important part of designing a national freight data architecture is to identify who the users are as well as their corresponding data needs. As previously mentioned, users include the community of public and private decisionmakers at the national, state, regional, and local levels.

The topic of freight data uses and needs has been widely covered in the literature through various reports, papers, peer exchanges, and conferences. A short sample of recent events and publications follows:

- 2001 Conference on Data Needs in the Changing World of Logistics and Freight Transportation, Saratoga Springs, NY (5);
- 2003 TRB *Special Report 276: A Concept for a National Freight Data Program* (4);
- 2004 draft BTS report "A Preliminary Roadmap for the American Freight Data Program" (13);
- 2005 Freight Data for State Transportation Agencies Peer Exchange, Boston, MA (125);
- 2005 New York Metropolitan Transportation Council (NYMTC) report "Description of Transportation Data to be Collected for NYMTC's Products, Reports, and Performance Measures" (126);
- 2007 Meeting Freight Data Challenges Workshop, Chicago, IL (127); and
- 2009 North American Freight Flows Conference: Understanding Changes and Improving Data Sources, Irvine, CA (128).

The focus of, and resulting recommendations from, these reports varied. For example, the 2001 Saratoga Springs conference focused on freight movements and recommended identifying freight data gaps, using data synthesis tools to fill data gaps, and developing performance measures for freight (5). This conference did not produce a list of data needs, although

it did highlight the need for finer resolution O-D data. The 2003 TRB *Special Report 276* concluded that providing all the data needed to satisfy all applications would be beyond the scope of any national initiative and recommended the following data items to capture important characteristics of freight movements (4):

- Origin and destination;
- Commodity characteristics, weight, and value;
- Modes of shipment;
- Routing and time of day; and
- Vehicle/vessel type and configuration.

The 2004 BTS report discussed the availability and limitation of various data sources and proposed a data collection program within BTS's American Freight Data Program (AFDP), as shown in Figure 7 (13).

The 2005 report on state data needs included the results of a survey of state agencies, which included the following in terms of freight data used and/or needed by states (based on responses from 14 states) (125):

- Business directories;
- Commodity characteristics, weight, and value;
- Congestion and travel time data;
- Crash and fatality data;
- Data on domestic versus international shipments within state;
- Economic, land use, and employment data;
- Hazardous material identifiers;
- Modal inventories;
- O-D data;
- Performance measure data;
- Real-time operational data;
- Routing and time of day;
- Truck and rail volume counts, classification, and weight;
- Vehicle and vessel types and configurations;

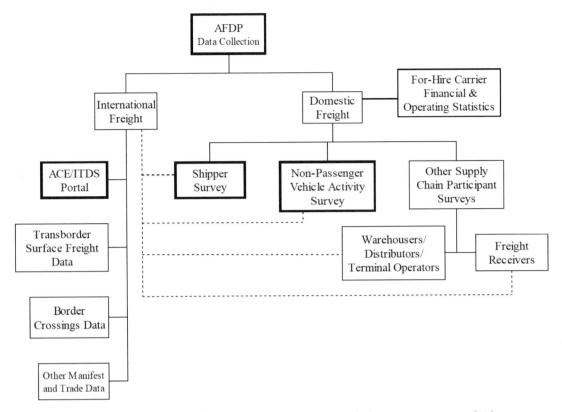

Figure 7. Freight data collection under the American Freight Data Program (13).

- Waybill data; and
- Weigh station data.

The NYMTC report on transportation data requirements produced a listing of data elements needed to support the needs of a variety of agencies in the New York metropolitan area (126). A summary of freight-related data requirements at NYMTC follows:

- Truck data:
  - Truck volumes (with respect to total traffic volumes);
  - Levels of service (LOS) for major truck routes;
  - Average speed;
  - Toll costs;
  - Curbside space management (loading/unloading zones, parking enforcement);
  - Accident and incident rates;
  - Height clearances;
  - Turning radii;
  - Access width;
  - Weight limitations;
  - Truck delays at railroad/highway grade crossings;
  - Usable shoulders;
  - Highway design standards, acceleration and deceleration lanes, truck climbing lanes;
  - Signage; and
  - Curbside capacity (for truck operations).

- Rail data:
  - Rail carloads exchanged with East of Hudson origins/destinations;
  - Container or trailer groundings in the East of Hudson region;
  - Rail freight levels of service (proprietary information, may be difficult to acquire);
  - Rail as a percentage of total regional freight traffic;
  - Number of competing carriers (preserving service options through future mergers);
  - Number of access modes (truck, barge/ferry);
  - Number of alternative access truck routes;
  - Connection time/distance to nearest limited-access highway or mainline rail head; and
  - Average cost of dray operations.
- Port data:
  - Actual throughput (total and per acre);
  - Actual throughput as a percentage of theoretical "maximum practical capacity" by functional component of each terminal (wharf and crane operation, storage, gate);
  - Average cargo dwell time;
  - Hours of terminal operation;
  - Utilization of storage (high versus low density);
  - Number of access modes (truck, rail, barge/ferry);
  - Rail barge mode share;
  - Number of alternative access truck routes;
  - LOS on major truck access routes;

- Access to on-dock rail;
- Connection time/distance to nearest limited-access highway or mainline rail head; and
- Average cost of dray operations.
- Air cargo data:
  - Aircraft parking;
  - Airfield capacity;
  - Warehouse capacity;
  - Availability/efficiency of federal inspection services;
  - Tug distance to aircraft parking ramp;
  - Number of alternative access truck routes;
  - Connection time/distance to nearest limited-access highway or central business district (CBD);
  - Average cost of dray; and
  - Operations.

The 2009 North American Freight Flows Conference: Understanding Changes and Improving Data Sources, Irvine, CA (128), included a number of presentations that further highlighted data needs and uses by a wide range of freight data users, including national-level agencies, states, regions, and the private sector. Worth noting were presentations that reported on the increasing use of fine-resolution Global Positioning System (GPS) data from truck fleets for the production of maps and reports documenting truck travel times, delays, and O-D patterns. Also worth noting was the increasing importance of accurate, appropriate data to support the growing demands for efficiency and productivity in the supply chain, particularly considering trends such as the increasing use of intermodal arrangements, the need to restructure distribution networks to maximize efficiency and minimize miles, and the need to make freight transportation more environmentally neutral.

Surveys and Interviews

For completeness, the research team conducted three sets of surveys to gather information about freight data uses and needs: A general survey, which focused on planners and analysts; a shipper survey; and a motor carrier survey. In general, the purpose of the surveys was twofold: (1) to gather general information about freight data practices and needs to confirm and/or expand the observations from the literature review and (2) to identify potential responders for more in-depth follow-up telephone interviews. Readers should be aware that the surveys and follow-up interviews were not random or scientific samples.

Planners and Analysts

The purpose of this activity was to gather information from government planners, analysts, and other similar freight-related stakeholders. The invitation to participate in the survey

included groups such as AASHTO committees, TRB committees, and AMPO. Not including forwarded e-mails, a rough estimate suggests that some 1,500 individuals received an invitation to participate. In total, 92 respondents completed the survey, with the following overall distribution:

- State agencies (32 percent),
- MPOs (22 percent),
- Federal agencies (11 percent),
- Ports (4 percent),
- Consultants (13 percent), and
- Other (18 percent).

Respondents were involved in all modes of transportation, including air, rail, truck, pipelines, and water. The research team contacted 22 online survey respondents for follow-up interviews.

General trends and observations from the survey responses and follow-up interviews include the following:

- Not surprisingly (given that respondents were typically planners), most respondents indicated that they use freight data to support the production of public-sector transportation planning documents. However, respondents also reported using freight data for a variety of other applications. Examples of freight data applications reported included the following:
  - Customs processing;
  - Development and economic incentives;
  - Economic analysis and impact;
  - Energy and climate change;
  - Environmental impacts and air quality conformance;
  - Goods movement;
  - Hazardous material handling;
  - Incident response;
  - Industry and state needs;
  - International trade;
  - Logistics management;
  - Marketing and seeking grant funding;
  - Planning and forecasting;
  - Performance measurement;
  - Policy development;
  - Regional and national system functionality analysis;
  - Roadside safety inspection;
  - Routing and dispatching;
  - Safety analysis;
  - Transportation infrastructure analysis, design, and construction;
  - Transportation operations;
  - Truck volumes for highway assignments; and
  - Workforce development and training.

  These trends add weight to the notion that the national freight data architecture should support the use of freight data for a wide range of applications, not just those in connection with traditional transportation planning and forecasting activities.

- With the exception of insurance statistics (which only had two responses), all other freight data types included in the survey were well represented in the responses. This trend is consistent with the observation above in that a variety of freight data options are necessary to support the various business processes in which planners are involved. Respondents also provided examples of freight data types not originally included in the survey. Examples of types of freight data identified by respondents included the following:
  - Business directories;
  - Commodity inventories;
  - Distribution warehouse truck traffic data;
  - Economic data;
  - Emissions estimates;
  - Employment by freight activity;
  - Fuel statistics;
  - GPS and GIS data;
  - Import/export statistics;
  - Infrastructure inventories;
  - Licensed carrier data;
  - Manifests and waybills;
  - Mine output data;
  - Operational data;
  - O-D data;
  - Oversize/overweight permits;
  - Pavement and infrastructure conditions;
  - Pipeline volumes;
  - Railroad tonnage data;
  - Safety data;
  - Speeds, travel times, and delays;
  - Traffic bottlenecks;
  - Vehicle inventories; and
  - Vehicle and traffic statistics.
- All of the freight data sources included in the survey were represented in the responses. Respondents also provided examples of freight data sources not originally included in the survey. Examples of freight data sources identified by respondents included the following:
  - Annual advisory group input,
  - Annual carrier meetings,
  - CFS,
  - EDI service providers,
  - Energy Data Book,
  - FAF,
  - FARS,
  - Freight transportation and logistics service,
  - General Estimates System (GES),
  - GPS data from trucks,
  - HPMS,
  - In-house roadway loop data,
  - LTL commodity/market flow database,
  - National Bridge Inventory,
  - NIPA,
  - NSDI,
  - North American Trucking Survey,
  - Own operational data,
  - Own regional forecasts of commodity volumes,
  - PIERS,
  - Private dataset from telematics network,
  - State estimates of truck traffic,
  - North American Transborder Freight Database,
  - TRANSEARCH Insight,
  - VIUS,
  - VTRIS, and
  - WCUS.
- The survey and follow-up interviews provided important feedback regarding unmet freight data needs (i.e., freight-related data that stakeholders do not currently have but would see benefit in having). Common unmet data needs expressed by respondents included the following:
  - Continuously updated or near real-time freight-related data;
  - Data that can be used to shed light on the economic impact of freight moving through a specific area or corridor;
  - Data that can be easily converted to reflect an accurate number of vehicles moving through a specific area or corridor;
  - Detailed routing information;
  - Freight transportation and inventory costs;
  - Idling statistics and accurate emissions data;
  - More accurate data, particularly economic data, O-D data (including external flows), and travel time and delay data;
  - More accurate employment data;
  - More affordable freight data (the complaint being that some private-sector databases are too expensive);
  - More cooperation among agencies that collect and disseminate freight-related data;
  - More data from private industry sources, particularly shippers and carriers, including vehicle-related data (e.g., GPS data), commodity data (e.g., waybills, manifests), and commercial vehicle availability by establishment;
  - More disaggregated commodity flow data (e.g., at the county level);
  - More accurate intermodal data;
  - O-D data beyond intermodal drayage for port-related trucks;
  - Percentage of total truck movements on local and regional systems that is actually port-related;
  - Rail traffic data;
  - Reintroduce VIUS;

- Standardized definitions and methodologies for collecting and disseminating transportation-related data;
- Truck volumes generated by local industrial and commercial sites and what implications those volumes have on determining the most desirable routes;
- Up-to-date national and state freight data; and
- Updated international O-D data.

Shippers

The purpose of this activity was to gather general information from the shipper community regarding freight data uses and needs, as well as willingness to share data with other freight-related stakeholders. The research team contacted representatives of 14 companies of various sizes, including third-party logistics, freight forwarders, manufacturers, retailers, and suppliers, and used the shipper questionnaire as a starting point for the discussion. Several industries and commodities were represented, including automobile parts, medical instruments, food and bakery products, chemical products, retail, furniture, and household cleaning products.

General trends and observations from this activity include the following:

- The shipper industry collects large amounts of data, particularly on a shipment-by-shipment basis. Typical shipment data elements collected included the following:
  - Shipper address;
  - Consignee address;
  - Commodity description (some shippers provide more commodity details than others);
  - Piece and/or pallet count;
  - Weight;
  - Carrier used;
  - Shipment billing type (e.g., collect, prepaid, and third-party prepaid);
  - Shipment bill to (i.e., party paying for the freight movement);
  - Shipment rate;
  - Ship date; and
  - Delivery due date.
- Many shippers and logistics service providers have the capability to transmit data electronically using EDI technologies. These stakeholders use EDI regularly for load tendering, tracking, and freight payment purposes. Technology has advanced to the point where it is routine for data providers to be able to tailor the amount of data and level of data detail they provide to individual trading partners and carriers within the supply chain. These capabilities offer unique opportunities for freight data exchange. However, shipper-provided EDI data may not be sufficient for transportation planning applications unless carrier movement data are included. For example, although a data record might characterize a commodity being transported as well as origin and destination locations, the route data component may be missing if the carrier is not integrated into the shipper's data transactions.
- Although each private company interviewed functioned differently, most companies keep freight-related data for similar purposes. The most common reasons for keeping data included the following:
  - Required by law or company policy to keep record of each shipment;
  - Accounting purposes;
  - Customer compliance;
  - Performance monitoring purposes;
  - Forecasting purposes;
  - Identifying new business opportunities (i.e., sales leads); and
  - Customs processing.
- Selection of freight mode of transportation is typically based on one or more of the following factors:
  - Freight bill payer's preference (typically, whoever pays for the freight selects the routing method);
  - Physical access characteristics of shipper and receiver locations;
  - Cost of the freight movement on a particular mode; and
  - Time sensitivity of the delivery process.
- Many respondents indicated they could not comment on their companies' ability or willingness to share data for freight transportation planning purposes without a higher-level executive's permission. This type of response is not surprising given the competitive nature of the shipping industry and the sensitive and/or confidential nature of some of the information those companies need to manage on a day-to-day basis. Subsequent feedback obtained at the peer exchange (see below) highlighted a number of strategies to address this issue, including initiating discussions about data sharing with industry associations to provide filtered and/or aggregated data. This strategy would enable individual firms to maintain confidentiality and would shield them from potential Freedom of Information Act requirements. A business model might also emerge in which data providers would forward sample data to a designated agency on a pre-determined schedule for developing a commodity flow database at the national level. The data would be stripped of certain identifiers to address privacy and confidentiality concerns. Although the data would not be available for free (since filtering, forwarding, storing, and processing the data would involve real costs), it is anticipated that the cost of collecting the data would be a fraction of the cost to conduct normal surveys.

Motor Carriers

The research team conducted a motor carrier survey and follow-up interviews to gather general and detailed information from the motor carrier community regarding private-sector freight data uses and needs, as well as willingness to share data with external freight-related stakeholders. The research team emailed survey solicitations to 75 for-hire interstate motor carriers of various sizes, which are members of an industry council on information and technology. In total, 13 motor carriers completed the online survey. The team conducted additional follow-up interviews with these respondents to supplement the survey results and glean insights into specific data elements collected by motor carriers. Survey respondents represented all major sectors of the carrier industry and had the following distribution: 46 percent TL, 23 percent LTL, and 31 percent specialized.

In general, motor carriers collect large amounts of data from a variety of sources, such as transportation management systems (TMSs), engine control modules (ECMs), freight billing and accounting, and in-cab communication systems including GPS-based systems and on-board safety systems. At a high level, the research team found that data collected by motor carriers that would be most relevant to a national freight data architecture fell into the following categories:

- Shipment level detail and tonnage;
- Vehicle routing and mileage; and
- Corporate revenue, profitability, and lane (corridor) analysis.

For all three major sectors of the industry (TL, LTL, and specialized), shipment-level data typically collected by motor carriers include shipper and consignee-related data such as name, address, shipper bill of lading number, freight rate or revenue detail, and pickup date. Less commonly collected shipment-level data include commodity-related description, shipment weight, tare-level data (e.g., pallet, drum, and pieces), delivery date, and shipper or shipment reference numbers.

Respondents stated that industry operating environments, customer expectations, and freight billing practices significantly affect the collection of shipment-level data by carriers. For example, TL carriers tend to bill customers on a per-mile basis or using a flat rate. Because the amount of revenue is the same regardless of shipment volume or weight, there is little incentive to collect commodity-level detailed data. TL carriers that do collect this type of data tend to collect only generalized, non-standardized, and/or proprietary descriptions. Interviewees also indicated that shipper bills of lading vary widely in commodity-level descriptions (or contain no description at all). In addition, TL carriers responded that they are less likely to collect data on tonnage hauled or tare-level data, also attributable to industry-accepted billing practices.

In contrast, LTL carriers stated that they were more likely to collect commodity-level detailed data. These carriers typically bill customers using a rate structure based on shipment weight, origin, destination, and freight classification. The traditional classification of LTL freight is based on NMFC codes. However, due to deregulation and the competitive landscape of the trucking industry, there is anecdotal evidence that LTL carriers are now collecting less descriptive or uniform commodity-level detailed data. It is common for freight rate negotiations between LTL carriers and shippers to result in a freight-all-kinds (FAK) rating structure that assigns a general freight classification to all shipments from a shipper regardless of freight commodity or type. LTL carriers also are more likely to track total tonnage, probably because carriers need to use more complicated profitability models, as well as labor productivity analyses, at cross dock or terminal locations.

Specialized carriers indicated that their collection of commodity-level detail depends highly on the specific type of freight or carrier operations. For example, carriers that transport a significant amount of hazardous materials are likely to collect detailed commodity-level data due to strict regulatory reporting requirements. Other specialized carriers (e.g., flat bed or heavy equipment haulers) may levy freight charges on a per-mile or flat rate basis, decreasing the need to collect shipment-level detailed data such as commodity or shipment weight.

A significant portion of the industry collects vehicle routing and mileage data. However, respondents indicated a discrepancy between actual routes traveled by company trucks and the recommended routes generated by truck management software packages. Due to the high per-mile costs of operating a truck, most carriers collect data on total fleet miles or average miles per truck. Coupled with revenue per shipment data, carriers also use mileage data to conduct lane and profitability analyses.

Most carriers interviewed do not participate in data sharing programs with public- or private-sector entities. However, all but one carrier indicated a willingness to share at least some type of data for public transportation planning activities. Nearly half of interviewees indicated that they would be willing to share data in aggregated form, while half indicated that they were not sure if they would be willing to share data. Common concerns expressed by interviewees regarding data sharing include the following:

- Carrier efforts to provide data must not be overly burdensome or cause the carrier to incur additional costs.
- It is critical to maintain the confidentiality and proprietary nature of the data. Data requests must also include clear provisions to protect the anonymity of both carriers and their customers.
- Carriers would need to know in advance the specific uses of the data. In return for sharing data, carriers would like some type of industry benchmarking metrics.

It is worth noting that developing metrics of interest to the private sector is part of NCFRP Project 3, "Performance Measures for Freight Transportation" (*129*). This project is developing measures to gauge the performance of the freight transportation system in areas such as capacity, safety, security, infrastructure condition, congestion, and operations. The measures should support investment, operations, and policy decisions by a range of stakeholders, both public and private, and reflect local, regional, national, and global perspectives.

Peer Exchange

In conjunction with the 2009 North American Freight Flows Conference in Irvine, CA (*128*), the research team organized a peer exchange to discuss preliminary research findings; request feedback; and facilitate a dialogue on implementation strategies to develop, adopt, and maintain a national freight data architecture.

As Figure 8 shows, the peer exchange included an opening session, breakout sessions, and a final group discussion session.

NCFRP Project 12 – Freight Data Architecture Peer Exchange
Thursday, September 17, 2009, 1:00 pm – 5:00 pm, Beckman Center

Background
The Texas Transportation Institute (TTI) is conducting research for NCFRP to (a) develop specifications for the content and structure of a freight data architecture that serves the needs of public and private decisionmakers at the national, state, and local levels; (b) identify the value and challenges of the potential architecture; and (c) recommend institutional strategies to develop and maintain the architecture.

Decisionmakers must understand the freight transportation system (including use, roles, and limitations) to respond to the growing logistical requirements of businesses and households. This understanding draws on disparate data sources—collected under various definitions, time scales, and geographic levels—such as commodity movements, relationships among sectors of the economy, international trade, traffic operations, supply chains, and infrastructure characteristics and conditions. Several studies and conferences call for a national freight data architecture to link existing datasets and guide new data collection programs. However, none of these calls defines what a data architecture is or how an architecture would be designed, implemented, or evaluated.

Peer Exchange Purpose
The purpose of the peer exchange is to discuss preliminary research findings; request feedback; facilitate a dialogue on architecture structure and components; and identify implementation strategies and challenges.

Preliminary Agenda
1:00 – 1:15 Welcome, introductions, and peer exchange objectives
1:15 – 2:00 Presentation of the draft interim report findings
2:00 – 2:15 Breakout group organization and instructions

2:15 – 4:00 Breakout groups (depending on the number of attendees)
    Group A: Freight data sources and data standards
    Group B: Developing an architecture for freight data
    Group C: Strategies and challenges for implementation

    2:15 – 2:45 Review research findings
    2:45 – 3:00 Coffee break
    3:00 – 3:30 Identify and prioritize needs
    3:30 – 4:00 Review and identify specification requirements

4:00 – 4:30 Reports from breakout groups
4:30 – 4:45 Group discussion and synthesis
4:45 – 5:00 Closing remarks, next steps, and wrap-up

Contact and Additional Information
Cesar Quiroga   Phone: (210) 731-9938   Email: c-quiroga@tamu.edu
Juan Carlos Villa   Phone: (979) 862-3382   E-mail: j-villa@tamu.edu
Texas Transportation Institute, Texas A&M University System

Figure 8. Peer exchange agenda.

56

The purpose of the opening session was to provide an overview of the research project and draft research findings. The purpose of the breakout sessions was to discuss findings and issues in more detail. The purpose of the final group discussion session was to exchange breakout session findings and summarize recommendations.

In total, 33 participants (representing federal, state, region, university, and private sectors) attended the peer exchange. Originally, the peer exchange included three breakout groups (Figure 8). However, breakout Group B was canceled because of low interest from peer exchange participants. As a result, relevant questions and issues for discussion were re-assigned to the other two breakout groups.

To encourage participation and discussion, attendees received background materials such as relevant research topic summaries and breakout group agendas and discussion objectives. Feedback from peer exchange participants included recommendations for changes to initial research findings (which were implemented) as well as a list of issues, challenges, and strategies to consider during the implementation of the national freight data architecture, which are summarized as follows:

- **Data at different geographic levels.** Participants thought the list of data sources discussed at the peer exchange was useful, but highlighted the need to include state, regional, and local data sources in the national freight data architecture, noting that national-level data are frequently inadequate for sub-state, local, corridor, and project analyses. For example, FAF and CFS regions are not consistent with MPO boundaries, making it difficult for MPOs to use national-level data. In addition, CFS is not designed to accept supplemental data from sources such as weigh-in-motion stations and routing permits. Participants considered county-level data collection to be more appropriate than state-level data collection (although some counties are very large). Discussion also included data collection at the three-digit zip code level.
- **Data at different levels of compatibility.** Participants noted that some datasets could be integrated more easily than other datasets. This observation led to a discussion about which datasets to include in a data architecture. Integrating spatial data (e.g., through conflation) is frequently possible if the geographic levels of resolution are compatible. However, other datasets are too dissimilar, making data integration considerably more difficult. A critical element in integrating datasets is a determination of how feasible it is to "integrate" each dataset into the system.
- **Freight data architecture vision.** Participants agreed that a national freight data architecture should provide a generic framework while providing a methodology to cross-reference data located within different databases and, at

the same time, addressing confidentiality concerns by all stakeholders involved. The data architecture should be dynamic rather than static, and be able to respond to new types of data, instead of just working with existing data. Participants also highlighted that a national freight architecture would need to work with cross-border data, and have the ability to include Canada and Mexico (i.e., be multinational with a North American scope). In addition, the national freight data architecture should support criteria and methods to locate, map, and classify freight trip generators, trip receivers, and other factors (e.g., employment, land use, ports, intermodal facilities, and airports).

The freight data architecture would also need to promote data harmonization (i.e., although datasets do not need to be located in the physical database, they need to have a common thread and comply with at least a minimum set of standards to facilitate data sharing and integration). Data harmonization standards need to include basic elements as spatial referencing metadata, in addition to complex elements as performance tracking data.

- **Freight data architecture value.** The value of a national freight data architecture would be demonstrated by the ability of stakeholders to make decisions on infrastructure projects and to the extent that business processes and data access become more efficient. The value also would be demonstrated by the level of support the data architecture provides to the implementation of freight performance measures. Participants discussed the monetary value of the data architecture. Although there was no consensus on how to manage that value, there was discussion about the need for consistent benefit/cost analysis standards and the need to identify the value of freight datasets, especially near-real-time commodity data and routing data. Participants also recommended the development of metrics to determine the effectiveness of implementing the data architecture.
- **Freight data architecture ownership.** Participants considered that the ownership and/or leadership role of a national freight data architecture would be best placed at the federal level, in principle, at RITA-BTS.
- **Private-sector data.** Participants acknowledged the difficulty in obtaining data from the private sector, but recommended leaving the door open for data-sharing participation and collaboration. Participants also recommended providing a strong message to the private sector that existing freight data issues affect both the public and private sectors. Participants highlighted the importance of contacting the right person at a sufficiently high administrative level for discussions about data access and sharing (since low-ranking personnel might know the data, but frequently do not have the authority or permission to discuss data-sharing options). It may be strategic to involve

trade associations rather than individual firms because trade associations can speak for the industry more easily and can provide leadership for starting a data-sharing relationship. Inviting the private sector to participate in the development of the freight data architecture would also help all of the parties understand issues of mutual concern and identify potential opportunities, especially if the result is lower costs and operational improvements.

- **Strategies for developing the freight data architecture.** Participants agreed with the concept of a scalable freight data architecture that can be implemented in phases (see Chapter 4), and highlighted that implementing a comprehensive data architecture at once with no testing of options prior to making a decision about the correct approach would be too risky. Participants also favored the concept of developing and comparing several alternative approaches.

Participants thought NCFRP would be a good avenue for funding the development of alternative data architecture concepts and a prototype. Participants indicated the request for proposals should outline clear objectives, while leaving the definition of approaches to the research team(s) selected. An idea discussed was to develop the data architecture around scenarios or themes, such as business areas or processes, levels of government, and/or economic activity. Participants identified four potential scenarios or themes, including MPOs, the private sector, cross-border trade (e.g., Washington State and British Columbia, or Texas and Mexico), and multistate freight (e.g., I-95 corridor, Great Lakes region). Activities and requirements in connection with each of these scenarios or themes would include structuring a competition for research teams (each of which would include a university partner, a private-sector partner, and a government-level partner) to develop and test competing data architecture concepts, making sure to include multimodal components in the scenarios and tests, and conduct a follow-up evaluation. The final step would be to merge the best concepts and practices into one composite program.

Other strategies for developing the data architecture included adding a communication or marketing component as well as identifying buy-in and consensus issues, compliance options, and an administration-level champion. Additional ideas discussed included developing a "showcase" to bring attention to the issue of freight data and developing a roadmap for collaboration between the public sector and the private sector for more effective data collection.

CHAPTER 4

Outline and Requirements for a National Freight Data Architecture

Introduction

This chapter provides a catalog of components, characteristics, and draft specifications for a national freight data architecture that takes into consideration the results and lessons learned from the literature review, surveys and follow-up interviews, and peer exchange described in Chapters 2 and 3.

Special Considerations

A prerequisite for the development of specifications for a national freight data architecture is to define what a national freight data architecture should be. There are several dimensions to this issue, including focus, content, scope, and access to private-sector data sources.

Freight Data Focus

Different stakeholders may have different interpretations of what should be the focus of the national freight data architecture. As such, focus affects content and, therefore, data architecture specifications. For example, a data architecture that focuses on commodity flows has certain data requirements such as O-D data; commodity characteristics, weight, and value; modes of shipment; routing and time of day; and vehicle type and configuration. By comparison, a data architecture that focuses on the physical interaction between commercial vehicles and the transportation network has different data needs, such as vehicle type and configuration, network characteristics and performance, oversize and overweight data, safety data, and inspection data. Likewise, a data architecture that focuses on commodity flows and requires the collection of real-time supply chain data from the private sector has special data confidentiality requirements. There is some overlap between different focus options, and the challenge is to identify which one(s) to pursue.

Freight Data Content

Different stakeholders may have different interpretations of what should be the content of (i.e., what should be included in) a national freight data architecture. As with focus, content affects data architecture specifications. Obviously, the content of a data architecture depends on what is meant by data architecture. Different definitions exist, but, in general, a data architecture is the manner and process used to organize and integrate data components. It is worth noting that a data architecture is not a database (databases may be built based on data architectures); a data model, a data standard, a specification, or a framework (these items could be components of a data architecture); a system architecture (a system architecture could use data architecture components); a simulation or optimization model; or an institutional program. In order to conceptualize data components, data architectures normally use one or more of the following tools:

- Business process model (i.e., a representation of processes);
- Conceptual model (i.e., a representation of concepts and relationships);
- Logical model (i.e., a representation of data characteristics and relationships that is independent of any physical implementation);
- Physical model (i.e., a representation of data characteristics and relationships that depends on the specific physical platform chosen for its implementation); and
- Data dictionary and/or metadata (i.e., listing of definitions, characteristics, and other properties of entities, attributes, and other data elements).

In practice, which tools to use in a data architecture depends on the purpose and needs of the specific application. For example, a data architecture can be generic or specific. An example of a data architecture that is tightly integrated into a specific application is the EFM data architecture (*130*). The EFM database schema includes several tables that support shipment tracking across the supply chain. By comparison, a generic data architecture that focuses on data flows rather than how data entities are organized and stored in a database is the National ITS Architecture (*87*). This architecture describes functions, subsystems where the functions reside, and data flows that connect functions and subsystems in connection with the implementation of transportation operation systems. It may be interesting to note that despite the name, National ITS Architecture implementations are usually carried out at the local level.

Freight Data Scope

Freight data scope (including both coverage and resolution) also has an impact on data architecture specifications. As documented in Chapter 3, different levels of decisionmaking tend to have different data requirements. For example, as the level of analysis migrates from a national level to a local level, the quantity and level of detail associated with the data needed for decisionmaking tends to increase. It follows that a data architecture that has to support several levels of decisionmaking has to accommodate a wider range of data requirements than does a data architecture that only needs to support one level of decisionmaking. By extension, a national data architecture that is to serve the needs of both public and private decisionmakers not just at the national level, but also at the state and local levels, has to be even more encompassing.

Plenty of documents provide information about the limitations of current data collection programs, adding weight to the idea that the coverage and resolution of current freight data sources are not sufficient. The data resolution issue is particularly critical because no statements are currently available that outline (1) the required data disaggregation and accuracy levels to address current and anticipated data collection needs from a technical and statistical perspective and (2) the corresponding impacts of those requirements on data collection costs and privacy requirements. Developing those statements is critical in order to identify data collection requirements (*131*).

Dimensions to freight data disaggregation include areas such as commodity type disaggregation, geographic disaggregation, temporal disaggregation, financial data disaggregation, operating data disaggregation, and privacy requirements. For example, CFS does not collect shipment data for certain industries and commodities and does not collect shipment data for shipments passing through the United States. In addition, cross-border shipment paths only include U.S. mileage. Further, CFS follows a 5-year cycle, which is inadequate for freight analyses in connection with phenomena such as recessions or droughts. The 2-year lag between data collection and release is also a weakness.

Likewise, the 2002 CFS used the largest 50 metropolitan areas plus remainders of state areas. Several ideas have been suggested to increase the number of CFS regions, including using three-digit zip codes (of which there are 929 throughout the country) and BEA areas (of which there are 172 throughout the country) (*37*). A recent study of techniques to generate national FAZs for transportation models recommended a system of 400 zones (*40*). A current NCFRP project (NCFRP Project 20, "Guidebook for Developing Sub-National Commodity Flow Data") is expected to shed light on recommended practices in this area (*132*). Specifically, the research will produce a guidebook describing standard procedures for compiling local, state, regional, and corridor commodity flow databases, as well as new and effective procedures for conducting sub-national commodity flow surveys and studies.

The need for data quality awareness is increasing, as evidenced by the 2001 OMB mandate that required Executive Branch agencies in charge of gathering, processing, or analyzing data for statistical purposes to issue quality guidelines to maximize the integrity, quality, and usability of the information those agencies disseminate (*133*). Relevant U.S.DOT documents include the HPMS field manual (*67*), the BTS compendium of source and accuracy statements (*76*), the *Guide to Good Statistical Practice in the Transportation Field* (*131*), and the *BTS Statistical Standards Manual* (*134*).

The privacy provisions in the E-Government Act of 2002 included a requirement for federal agencies to conduct privacy impact assessments (PIAs) to document what information is to be collected, its purpose and intended use, information sharing practices and security measures, opportunities for consent, and whether a system of records is created following Privacy Act provisions (*135*). The PIAs for the systems managed by the various operating administrations within the U.S.DOT, including relevant freight-related systems discussed in this report, are listed online (*136*).

Access to Private-Sector Data Sources

Aggregated freight data from commercial data providers have been available for years. For example, TRANSEARCH Insight merges several data sources including data from federal agencies and data from carriers. PIERS relies on data sources such as copies of shipping documents, monthly summaries from CBP, and information gathered through partnerships with companies abroad that specialize in manifest data collection in other countries. In practice, it is not always possible to obtain detailed documentation about the characteristics and methodology used for the production of commercial databases. These databases can be more expensive compared to public-sector data (at least from the standpoint of regular freight data users who do not need to internalize the cost to collect, process, and publish public-sector data).

The shipper industry collects large amounts of data. Many shippers and logistics service providers transmit data electronically using EDI technologies. These stakeholders use EDI regularly for load tendering, tracking, and freight payment purposes. However, accessing data from shippers and logistics service providers for transportation planning applications (beyond aggregated data from commercial data providers and national survey campaigns such as CFS) is not necessarily straightforward. For example, although a data record might characterize a commodity as well as origin and destination locations, the route data component may be missing unless the carrier movement data are included. In addition, many of the shipper stakeholders interviewed indicated they could not share data without the express consent of senior management and a review by their legal departments (particularly on a load-by-load basis, given its proprietary and confidential nature).

Motor carriers also expressed reservations about sharing proprietary and confidential data. Their reservations were related to the need to develop mechanisms to protect proprietary and confidential information and to maintain the anonymity of carriers and customers. In general, carriers would need to know in advance the specific uses of the data and, in return, would expect information in the form of industry benchmarking metrics. It is worth noting that developing metrics of interest to the private sector is part of NCFRP Project 3, "Performance Measures for Freight Transportation" (129).

In practice, the type and amount of data provided by, or available through, carriers varies considerably, depending on factors such as carrier size, geographic locations, activity focus, and type of cargo transported. Carriers handle large amounts of disaggregated data during the course of their business operations. Increasingly, carriers use EDI standards and applications. However, most of this information is confidential and limited to the direct exchange of data between trading partners. Some federal agencies are implementing EDI-based technologies to capture data from carriers, mainly through customs and homeland security processes.

The amount of shipment information detail in EDI transaction sets varies according to the type of transaction set used. In general, although the transaction sets support the use of commodity codes such as NMFC or STCC, these codes are different from other codes such as SCTG or NAPCS. Although crosswalk tables enable the conversion of commodity codes across coding systems, the current inventory of crosswalk tables is neither comprehensive nor coordinated. Questions also remain regarding the current level of market penetration

of standardized commodity codes among shippers and carriers because, in reality, industry operational environments, customer expectations, and freight billing practices affect the collection of shipment-level data by carriers. For example, TL carriers, who tend to bill customers on a per-mile basis or by using a flat rate, rarely collect detailed commodity data, collecting instead generalized, non-standardized, and/or proprietary descriptions. Shipper bills of lading also vary widely in commodity-level descriptions (or contain no description at all). In addition, TL carriers are less likely to collect data on tonnage hauled or tare-level data, also attributable to industry-accepted billing practices.

By comparison, LTL carriers typically bill customers using a rate structure based on shipment weight, origin, destination, and freight classification. As a result, they tend to collect more commodity-level data. The traditional classification of LTL freight is based on NMFC codes. However, there is anecdotal evidence that LTL carriers frequently collect less descriptive or uniform commodity-level detailed data, favoring a freight-all-kinds rating structure that assigns a general freight classification to all shipments from a shipper regardless of freight commodity or type. As opposed to TL carriers, LTL carriers are more likely to track total tonnage.

The implementation of ITS technologies is facilitating the acquisition of operational-level data from carriers. Most of these initiatives focus on the interaction between carriers and the transportation network environment, but not on the collection of detailed commodity data. This is the case of the CVISN program, which involves the deployment of systems to streamline the credential process, automate inspection screening activities, and exchange data in connection with safety checks, credential checks, and fee processing.

Some initiatives are addressing data exchange between stakeholders along the supply chain process, as in the case of the EFM initiative sponsored by FHWA, but it is not yet clear whether, and to what degree, some of the data resulting from this process could be used for freight transportation planning purposes. EFM has undergone several field tests, including field operational tests at O'Hare and JFK International Airports, and the Columbus Electronic Freight Management deployment test. An upcoming deployment test is scheduled to launch at the Kansas City SmartPort project.

Other initiatives also are resulting in the collection of vast amounts of operational-level data at little to no cost to carriers, as in the case of the FHWA-sponsored initiative that has resulted in the collection of several billion anonymized positional data records per year from more than 600,000 trucks that operate in North America. This large database is facilitating the determination of performance measures such as travel times and speeds on freight-significant highways, as well as route choice by truck drivers.

National Freight Data Architecture Definition

Based on the analysis in the previous section, a generic definition for a national freight data architecture is as follows:

> The national freight data architecture is the manner in which data elements are organized and integrated for freight transportation-related applications or business processes. The data architecture includes the necessary set of tools that describe related functions or roles, components where those roles reside or apply, and data flows that connect roles and components at different domain and aggregation levels.

In practice, several alternative implementation options may be possible depending on factors such as the following:

- What is the freight community really interested in pursuing?
- What is the level of funding that different stakeholders (both public and private) are willing to invest to support that effort?
- Where is the source of the funding and what are the requirements and steps to secure it?
- What benefits would different stakeholders derive?
- What is the implementation horizon?

There are no simple answers to these questions. Although this report lays out a few alternative implementation options and discusses issues such as value, challenges, and strategies to assist with the discussion, ultimately it is up to the freight community to decide what option to implement (and how). Some alternative implementation options follow:

- **Single-application approach.** In this case, the national freight data architecture would become the manner in which data elements are organized and integrated for *a specific* freight application or business process at the national level (e.g., commodity flows).
- **Intermediate approaches (depending on the number of applications).** In this case, the national freight data architecture would become the manner in which data elements are organized and integrated for *a specific set* of applications at the national, state, regional, and local levels. A large number of intermediate approaches is possible, depending on the business processes and geographic levels included. For example, an intermediate implementation approach could include commodity flows at the national, state, and regional levels. Another, more encompassing, intermediate implementation approach could include commodity flows, safety, and pavement impacts at the national, state, regional, and local levels.
- **Holistic, all-encompassing approach.** In this case, the national freight data architecture would become the manner in which data elements are organized and integrated for *all* freight transportation-related applications or business processes at the national, state, regional, and local levels.

For any of these implementation options, the data architecture would include the necessary set of tools that describe related functions or roles, components where those roles reside or apply, and data flows that connect roles and components.

National Freight Data Architecture Value

Increasing the focus, content, and scope of the national freight data architecture has the potential to increase the total benefit derived from its implementation (Figure 9a). However, the rate of growth of the total benefit would probably decrease with the level of implementation (and even become negative at some point). At the same time, the complexity and costs associated with the implementation of the national freight data architecture would be likely to increase with the level of implementation (Figure 9b). The value of the national freight data architecture is a function of both total benefit and cost and complexity associated with its implementation. As Figure 9c shows, it is quite likely that the maximum net value would take place at some intermediate level of implementation.

These observations suggest a scalable implementation path in which the national freight data architecture starts with one application at one or two levels of decisionmaking and then adds applications and levels of decisionmaking as needed or according to a predetermined implementation plan until, eventually, reaching the maximum net value. Unfortunately, data about benefits, costs, or complexity for each level of implementation that might enable a quantifiable determination of value are currently not available. Conducting appropriate benefit-cost analyses to obtain this type of information is a necessary activity that needs to occur both at the beginning and at different phases of implementation of the national freight data architecture.

From the documentation and information gathered in previous chapters, the research team identified the following list of benefits that, together, provide a statement of value for the national freight data architecture:

- Better understanding of the different business processes that affect freight transportation at different levels of coverage and resolution;
- Better understanding of the supply chain, which should help transportation planners to identify strategies for improving freight transportation infrastructure;
- Better understanding of the role that different public-sector and private-sector stakeholders play in freight transportation;

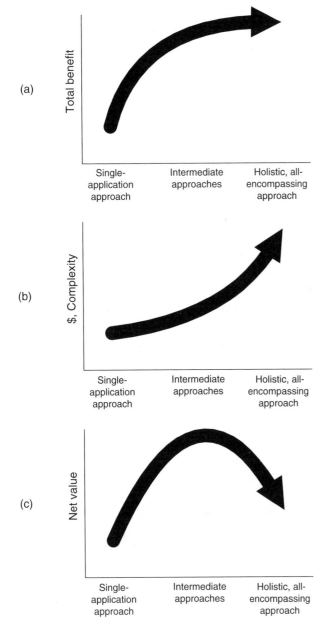

Figure 9. Relationship between national freight data architecture implementation level, total benefit, cost and complexity, and net value.

- Better understanding of the need for standards to assist in data exchange;
- Systematic, coordinated development of reference datasets (e.g., comprehensive commodity code crosswalk tables);
- Systematic inventory of freight transportation data sources;
- Systematic inventory of user and data needs that are prerequisites for the development of freight data management systems;
- Use as a reference for the identification of locations where there may be freight data redundancy and inefficiencies;

- Use as a reference for requesting funding allocations in the public and private sectors; and
- Use as a reference for the development of outreach, professional development, and training materials.

National Freight Data Architecture Components

As previously mentioned, a data architecture is not limited to data models because the models are just the tools that enable a systematic understanding of other components such as data, business processes, and roles. A list of components that make up a data architecture is therefore necessary. In the context of a scalable national freight data architecture that might need to serve the needs of a variety of decisionmaking levels, this data architecture would need to include a number of component categories, such as the following:

- Physical transportation components,
- Cargo or freight,
- Freight functions or roles,
- Business processes,
- Data sources,
- Freight-related data,
- Freight data models,
- Freight data standards, and
- User interface and supporting documentation.

This list is preliminary and will need to be refined during the process of developing and implementing the data architecture.

Figure 10 shows a high-level modular conceptualization and lists different categories of components. Each category and each component in Figure 10 can be thought of as an object or dimension that can be defined and characterized using appropriate information parameters such as description, domain, aggregation levels, attributes, and performance measures. Although the diagram emphasizes the high degree of interaction among components, the main use of the diagram would be as a tool to develop explicit lists of components to include in the national freight data architecture. As such, the diagram recognizes the scalable nature of the national freight data architecture and enables the production of a variety of diagram versions (as well as tabular representations) depending on what implementation level to pursue. For example, for a single-application data architecture that only focuses on commodity flows at the national level, it may not be necessary to depict (at least not in detail) other freight functions and business processes. Similarly, not all data standards would need to be considered, and the requirements for user interfaces to support that data architecture would be relatively minor. Figure 11 and Table 8 illustrate this concept.

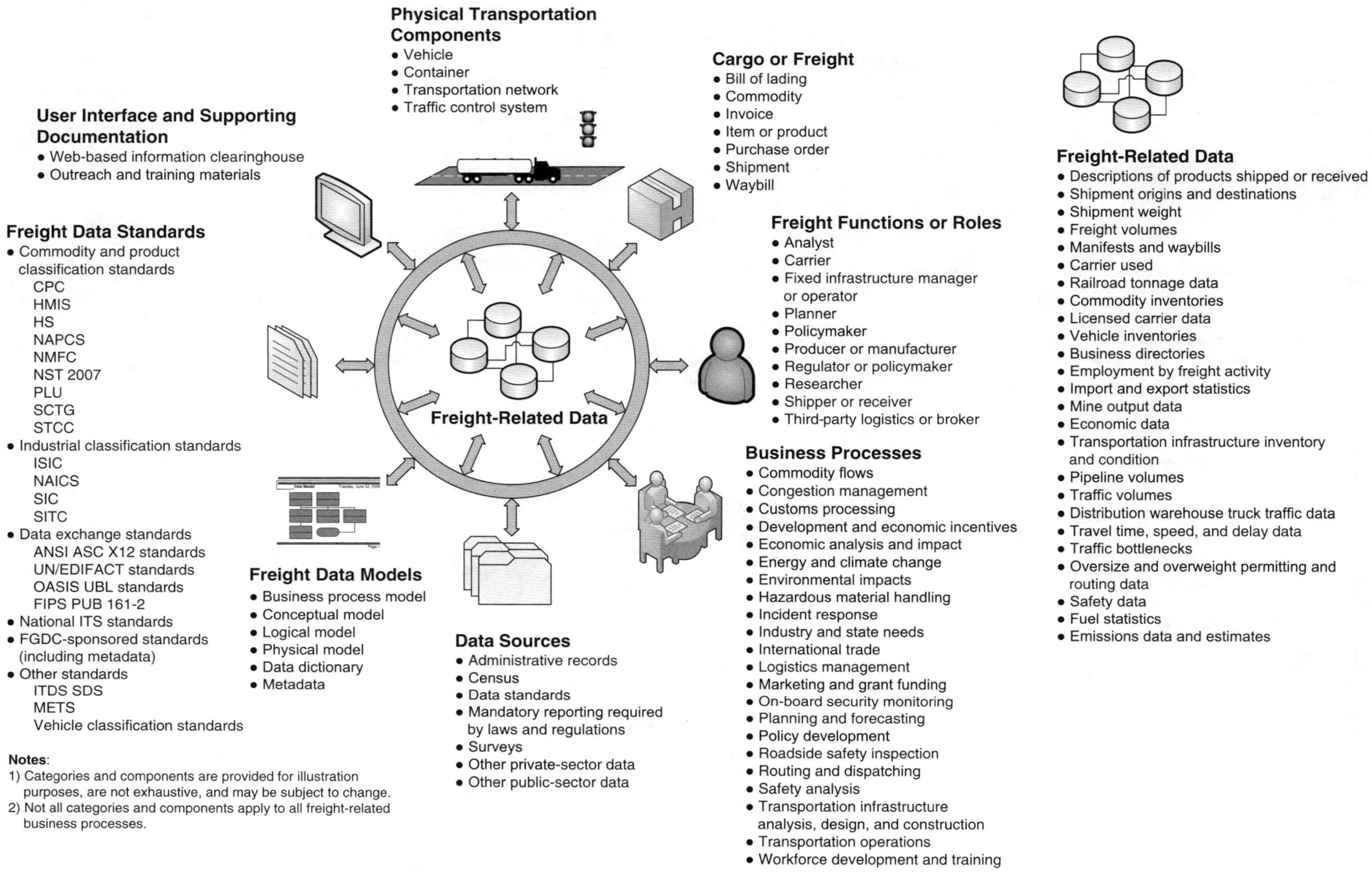

User Interface and Supporting Documentation
- Web-based information clearinghouse
- Outreach and training materials

Freight Data Standards
- Commodity and product classification standards
  - CPC
  - HMIS
  - HS
  - NAPCS
  - NMFC
  - NST 2007
  - PLU
  - SCTG
  - STCC
- Industrial classification standards
  - ISIC
  - NAICS
  - SIC
  - SITC
- Data exchange standards
  - ANSI ASC X12 standards
  - UN/EDIFACT standards
  - OASIS UBL standards
  - FIPS PUB 161-2
- National ITS standards
- FGDC-sponsored standards (including metadata)
- Other standards
  - ITDS SDS
  - METS
- Vehicle classification standards

Freight Data Models
- Business process model
- Conceptual model
- Logical model
- Physical model
- Data dictionary
- Metadata

Physical Transportation Components
- Vehicle
- Container
- Transportation network
- Traffic control system

Cargo or Freight
- Bill of lading
- Commodity
- Invoice
- Item or product
- Purchase order
- Shipment
- Waybill

Data Sources
- Administrative records
- Census
- Data standards
- Mandatory reporting required by laws and regulations
- Surveys
- Other private-sector data
- Other public-sector data

Freight Functions or Roles
- Analyst
- Carrier
- Fixed infrastructure manager or operator
- Planner
- Policymaker
- Producer or manufacturer
- Regulator or policymaker
- Researcher
- Shipper or receiver
- Third-party logistics or broker

Business Processes
- Commodity flows
- Congestion management
- Customs processing
- Development and economic incentives
- Economic analysis and impact
- Energy and climate change
- Environmental impacts
- Hazardous material handling
- Incident response
- Industry and state needs
- International trade
- Logistics management
- Marketing and grant funding
- On-board security monitoring
- Planning and forecasting
- Policy development
- Roadside safety inspection
- Routing and dispatching
- Safety analysis
- Transportation infrastructure analysis, design, and construction
- Transportation operations
- Workforce development and training

Freight-Related Data
- Descriptions of products shipped or received
- Shipment origins and destinations
- Shipment weight
- Freight volumes
- Manifests and waybills
- Carrier used
- Railroad tonnage data
- Commodity inventories
- Licensed carrier data
- Vehicle inventories
- Business directories
- Employment by freight activity
- Import and export statistics
- Mine output data
- Economic data
- Transportation infrastructure inventory and condition
- Pipeline volumes
- Traffic volumes
- Distribution warehouse truck traffic data
- Travel time, speed, and delay data
- Traffic bottlenecks
- Oversize and overweight permitting and routing data
- Safety data
- Fuel statistics
- Emissions data and estimates

Freight-Related Data (center of diagram)

Notes:
1) Categories and components are provided for illustration purposes, are not exhaustive, and may be subject to change.
2) Not all categories and components apply to all freight-related business processes.

Figure 10. National freight data architecture framework and components.

Physical Transportation Components

- ✓ Vehicle
- ✓ Container
- ✓ Transportation network
- Traffic control system

User Interface and Supporting Documentation

- ✓ Web-based information clearinghouse
- ✓ Outreach and training materials

Freight Data Standards

- Commodity and product classification standards
  - ✓ CPC
  - ✓ HMIS
  - ✓ HS
  - ✓ NAPCS
  - ✓ NMFC
  - ✓ NST 2007
  - ✓ PLU
  - ✓ SCTG
  - ✓ STCC
- Industrial classification standards
  - ISIC
  - ✓ NAICS
  - SIC
  - ✓ SITC
- Data exchange standards
  - ✓ ANSI ASC X12 standards
  - UN/EDIFACT standards
  - OASIS UBL standards
  - ✓ FIPS PUB 161-2
  - National ITS standards
  - FGDC-sponsored standards (including metadata)
- Other standards
  - ITDS SDS
  - METS
- Vehicle classification standards

Freight Data Models

- ✓ Business process model
- ✓ Conceptual model
- ✓ Logical model
- ✓ Physical model
- ✓ Data dictionary
- ✓ Metadata

Cargo or Freight

- ✓ Bill of lading
- ✓ Commodity
- Invoice
- ✓ Item or product
- ✓ Purchase order
- ✓ Shipment
- ✓ Waybill

Freight Functions or Roles

- ✓ Analyst
- ✓ Carrier
- Fixed infrastructure manager or operator
- ✓ Planner
- ✓ Policymaker
- ✓ Producer or manufacturer
- ✓ Researcher
- ✓ Shipper or receiver
- ✓ Third-party logistics or broker

Business Processes

- ✓ Commodity flows
- Congestion management
- Customs processing
- Development and economic incentives
- Economic analysis and impact
- Energy and climate change
- Environmental impacts
- Hazardous material handling
- Incident response
- Industry and state needs
- International trade
- Logistics management
- Marketing and grant funding
- On-board security monitoring
- Planning and forecasting
- Policy development
- Roadside safety inspection
- Routing and dispatching
- Safety analysis
- Transportation infrastructure analysis, design, and construction
- Transportation operations
- Workforce development and training

Data Sources

- ✓ Administrative records
- ✓ Census
- ✓ Data standards
- ✓ Mandatory reporting required by laws and regulations
- ✓ Surveys
- ✓ Other private-sector data
- ✓ Other public-sector data

Freight-Related Data

- ✓ Descriptions of products shipped or received
- ✓ Shipment origins and destinations
- ✓ Shipment weight
- ✓ Freight volumes
- ✓ Manifests and waybills
- Carrier used
- ✓ Railroad tonnage data
- Commodity inventories
- Licensed carrier data
- Vehicle inventories
- Business directories
- Employment by freight activity
- Import and export statistics
- Mine output data
- Economic data
- Transportation infrastructure inventory and condition
- ✓ Pipeline volumes
- ✓ Traffic volumes
- Distribution warehouse truck traffic data
- Travel time, speed, and delay data
- Traffic bottlenecks
- ✓ Oversize and overweight permitting and routing data
- Safety data
- Fuel statistics
- Emissions data and estimates

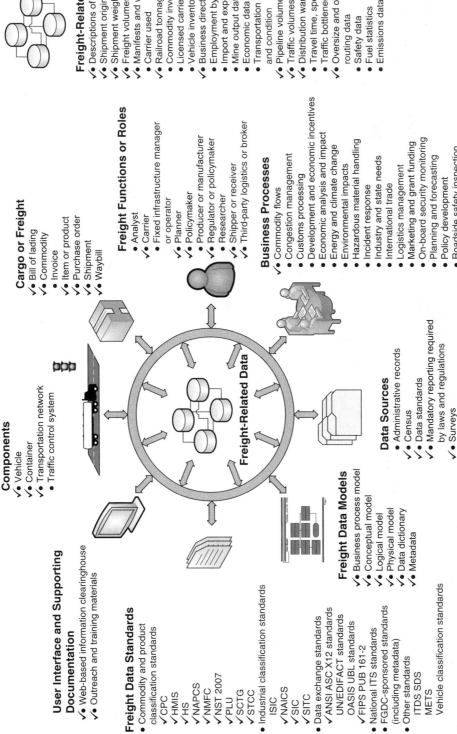

Freight-Related Data

Notes:

1) Categories and components are provided for illustration purposes, are not exhaustive, and may be subject to change.
2) Not all categories and components apply to all freight-related business processes.
3) Components marked with ✓ focus on commodity flows at the national level.

Figure 11. National freight data architecture components (focus on commodity flows at the national level).

Table 8. Category components that pertain to commodity flows at the national level.

National Freight Data Architecture Category/Component	Commodity-Flow-Related	National Freight Data Architecture Category/Component	Commodity-Flow-Related
Cargo or Freight		Travel time, speed, and delay data	
Bill of lading	•	Vehicle inventories	
Commodity	•	**Freight Data Model**	
Invoice		Business process model	•
Item or product	•	Conceptual model	•
Purchase order	•	Data dictionary	•
Shipment	•	Logical model	•
Waybill	•	Metadata	•
Physical Transportation		Physical model	
Container	•	**Freight Data Standard**	
Traffic control system	•	Commodity/product classification:	
Transportation network	•	CPC	•
Vehicle		HMIS	•
Freight Function or Role		HS	•
Analyst		NAPCS	•
Carrier	•	NMFC	•
Fixed infrastructure manager		NST 2007	•
Planner	•	PLU	•
Policymaker	•	SCTG	•
Producer or manufacturer		STCC	•
Regulator	•	Industrial classification standards:	
Researcher		ISIC	
Shipper or receiver	•	NAICS	•
Third-party logistics or broker	•	SIC	•
Freight-Related Data		SITC	•
Business directories	•	Data exchange standards:	
Carrier used		ANSI ASC X12 standard	•
Commodity inventories		FIPS PUB 161-2	•
Products shipped/received	•	OASIS UBL standards	
Distribution warehouse truck traffic	•	UN/EDIFACT standards	
Economic data		National ITS standards	
Emissions data and estimates		FGDC-sponsored standards	
Employment by freight activity		Other standards:	
Freight volumes	•	ITDS SDS	
Fuel statistics		METS	
Import and export statistics		Vehicle classification standards	
Licensed carrier data		**Data Source**	
Manifests and waybills	•	Administrative records	
Mine output data		Census	•
Oversize/overweight routing data	•	Data standards	•
Pipeline volumes	•	Mandatory reporting required by laws	•
Railroad tonnage data	•	Surveys	•
Safety data		Other private-sector data	•
Shipment origins and destinations	•	Other public-sector data	•
Shipment weight	•	**User interface/supporting documentation**	
Traffic bottlenecks		Outreach and training materials	•
Traffic volumes	•	Web information clearinghouse	•
Transportation infrastructure inventory			

Note: Components not marked as commodity-flow-related are not critical or may be considered optional.

The diagram in Figure 10 is only one example of potentially many different types of diagrams that can be used to depict interactions among freight transportation components. An example of a different type of diagram is Figure 12, which shows a high-level conceptual model that depicts relationships between different individual data architecture components for specific business processes. In Figure 12, each oval represents a component within a component category. For example, a physical transportation component could be a vehicle, a container, a transportation network, or a traffic control system.

Arrows between ovals represent relationships between components. Each component is associated with user interface and supporting documentation components (as indicated by the Documentation label). The arrows between ovals in Figure 12 represent many-to-many relationships between components. Examples of relationships include the following:

- A physical transportation component can be associated with many cargo or freight components and/or freight function or role components.

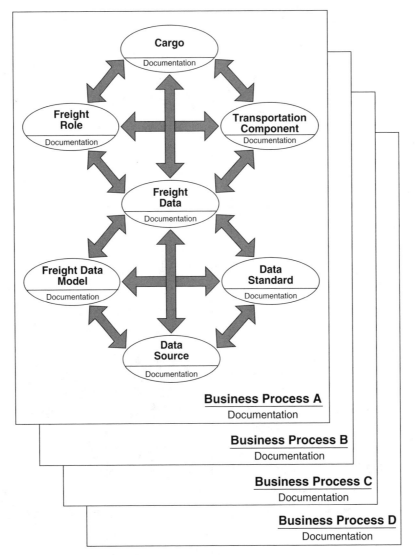

Figure 12. National freight data architecture component conceptual model.

- A cargo or freight component can be associated with many physical transportation components and/or freight functions or role components.
- A physical transportation component, a cargo or freight component, and a freight function or role component can produce freight-related data. Likewise, freight-related data can be associated with many physical transportation components, cargo or freight components, and/or freight function or role components.

National Freight Data Architecture Specifications

This section describes some of the most relevant specifications to implement and develop the various national freight data architecture components described in the previous section. Readers should note that the list of specifications is preliminary and might need refinement during the process of building the data architecture. The specifications described in this section are as follows:

- Compare candidate data architecture implementation concepts;
- Develop implementation plan for national freight data architecture components;
- Develop lists of components to include in the national freight data architecture;
- Develop and implement protocols for continuous stakeholder participation;
- Conduct data gap analysis;
- Conduct data disaggregation need analysis;
- Assume a distributed approach (as opposed to a centralized approach) to freight data repository implementations;
- Use a systems engineering approach for developing the national freight data architecture;
- Use standard information technology tools and procedures;

- Develop and/or use standardized terminology and definitions for each data architecture component developed;
- Implement strong privacy protection strategies; and
- Establish integration points with other data architectures and standards.

Compare Candidate Data Architecture Implementation Concepts

As previously mentioned, there are several potential implementation levels for a national freight data architecture, including the following:

- **Single-application approach.** In this case, the national freight data architecture would become the manner in which data elements are organized and integrated for *a specific* freight application or business process at the national level (e.g., commodity flows).
- **Intermediate approaches (depending on the number of applications).** In this case, the national freight data architecture would become the manner in which data elements are organized and integrated for *a specific set* of applications at the national, state, regional, and local levels.
- **Holistic, all-encompassing approach.** In this case, the national freight data architecture would become the manner in which data elements are organized and integrated for *all* freight transportation-related applications or business processes at the national, state, regional, and local levels.

It is not necessary to evaluate all of the candidate implementation levels. However, as the development of the National ITS Architecture demonstrated, comparing various data architecture concepts enabled the ITS community to develop a better understanding of the issues, which, in turn, facilitated the decision of which data architecture to pursue. In the case of the national freight data architecture, it is reasonable to expect a scalable implementation path that starts with one application at one or two levels of decisionmaking and then adds applications and levels of decisionmaking as needed or according to a predetermined implementation plan until, eventually, reaching the maximum net value. As previously mentioned, data about benefits, costs, or complexity for each level of implementation that might enable a quantifiable determination of value are currently not available. Conducting appropriate benefit-cost analyses to obtain this type of information is a necessary activity that needs to occur both at the beginning and at different phases of implementation of the national freight data architecture.

A peer exchange recommendation was to use NCFRP as a mechanism for funding the development of alternative data architecture concepts and prototype. Participants indicated the request for proposals should outline clear objectives, while leaving the definition of approaches to the research team(s)

selected. An idea discussed was to develop the data architecture around scenarios or themes, such as business areas or processes, levels of government, and/or economic activity. Participants identified four potential scenarios or themes, including MPOs, the private sector, cross-border trade (e.g., Washington State and British Columbia, or Texas and Mexico), and multistate freight (e.g., I-95 corridor, Great Lakes region). Activities and requirements in connection with each of these scenarios or themes would include structuring a competition for research teams (each of which would include a university partner, a private-sector partner, and a government-level partner) to develop and test competing data architecture concepts, making sure to include multimodal components in the scenarios and tests, and to conduct a follow-up evaluation. The final step would be to merge the best concepts and practices into one composite program.

Develop Implementation Plan for National Freight Data Architecture Components

Part of the analysis will include developing a plan for component implementation depending on the selected data architecture implementation level(s). The plan, which should include both short-term as well as long-term activities, will enable stakeholders to measure implementation progress and identify corrective actions if needed. The plan should include, at a minimum, the following activities:

- Develop lists of components to include in the national freight data architecture;
- Develop and implement protocols for continuous stakeholder participation;
- Conduct data gap analysis;
- Conduct data disaggregation need analysis;
- Develop, test, and validate data models; and
- Develop an implementation schedule, including both short-term as well as long-term activities.

This chapter describes some of these activities in detail.

Develop Lists of Components to Include in the National Freight Data Architecture

Following Figure 10, the national freight data architecture should include one or more of the following categories of components (depending on the results of the data architecture comparison analysis above):

- **Physical transportation components.** The physical transportation components refer to all the components used to transport cargo or freight. For each component, it will be necessary to identify the relevant data models to include in the data architecture, using as a reference existing systems

68

and databases. Examples of components (which could include subtypes to provide adequate disaggregation level support) include the following:
- Vehicle,
- Container,
- Transportation network, and
- Traffic control system.

A mode of transportation describes a functional combination of vehicles, containers, transportation network, and traffic control. Common modes of freight transportation in the United States are air, rail, truck, pipeline, and water. The developer should note that some applications (e.g., CFS and FAF) use special mode of transportation designations for intermodal movements that do not necessarily conform to the definition above. The national freight data architecture will need to handle these special cases at the data model level.

- **Cargo or freight.** Cargo or freight refers to the various components that describe the goods being transported. For each component, it will be necessary to identify the relevant data elements to include in the data architecture, using data elements already included in existing standards (e.g., EDI standards) as a reference. A small sample of components in this category, which could be expanded as needed, includes the following:
  - Bill of lading,
  - Commodity,
  - Invoice,
  - Item or product,
  - Purchase order,
  - Shipment, and
  - Waybill.
- **Freight functions or roles.** Freight functions or roles refer to the type of responsibility a stakeholder has in relation to freight transportation. Depending on the data architecture implementation level selected, this part of the analysis will include developing a map of functions and the typical kinds of freight data that each function requires. A situation in which this type of mapping is necessary is when trying to identify different levels of data access to different stakeholders. Examples of roles (which could include subtypes to provide adequate support for roles at different disaggregation levels) include the following:
  - Analyst,
  - Carrier,
  - Fixed infrastructure manager or operator,
  - Planner,
  - Policymaker,
  - Producer or manufacturer,
  - Regulator,
  - Researcher,
  - Shipper or receiver, and
  - Third-party logistics or broker.

- **Business processes.** Business processes refer to the various types of activities that different stakeholders have in relation to freight transportation. Depending on the data architecture implementation level selected, this part of the analysis will include developing formal representations of freight-related business processes using industry-standard business process modeling tools. Examples of high-level business processes (which could include subtypes to provide adequate support for business processes at different disaggregation levels) include the following:
  - Commodity flows;
  - Congestion management;
  - Customs processing;
  - Development and economic incentives;
  - Economic analysis and impact;
  - Energy and climate change;
  - Environmental impacts;
  - Hazardous material handling;
  - Incident response;
  - Industry and state needs;
  - International trade;
  - Logistics management;
  - Marketing and grant funding;
  - On-board security monitoring;
  - Planning and forecasting;
  - Policy development;
  - Roadside safety inspection;
  - Routing and dispatching;
  - Safety analysis;
  - Transportation infrastructure analysis, design, and construction;
  - Transportation operations; and
  - Workforce development and training.

One of the first activities while developing the national freight data architecture will be to assemble a prioritized list of business processes for implementation.
- **Data sources.** Data sources refer to systems, databases, data collection programs, reports, and other similar products and activities that can be sources of freight data. Examples of data sources (which could include subtypes to provide adequate support for data sources at different disaggregation levels) include the following:
  - Administrative records,
  - Census,
  - Data standards,
  - Mandatory reporting required by laws and regulations,
  - Surveys,
  - Other private-sector data, and
  - Other public-sector data.

It will be necessary to develop a properly cross-referenced index of data sources, using as a foundation already existing systems such as BTS's TranStats (*137*). One of the activities to complete will be to formulate recommendations for potential upgrades to TranStats to include other freight-related data sources, including state agencies and private-sector data sources. Based on experiences with other systems and architectures (e.g., the National ITS Architecture) one of the requirements in this area also will be to include archived freight data capabilities in the data architecture.

- **Freight-related data.** Freight-related data refer to the various types of data that can be associated with each of the components previously mentioned (i.e., physical transportation components, cargo or freight, business functions or roles, business processes, and data sources). Freight-related data can be associated with just one component or in connection with the interaction between two or more components. For example, in the supply chain, a product or order must have relevant information about different requirements, situations, and conditions that might influence the movement from origin to destination. This information is needed for a variety of reasons, including payment, shipment, safety and recall purposes, and documentation to affected stakeholders.

  Some of the most commonly used types of freight data, as well as types of freight data that users do not have but would see benefit in having, include the following (while developing the national freight data architecture, it will be necessary to assemble a comprehensive inventory of freight data types and prioritize those types for implementation):
  - Descriptions of products shipped or received;
  - Shipment origins and destinations;
  - Shipment weight;
  - Freight volumes;
  - Manifests and waybills;
  - Carrier used;
  - Railroad tonnage data;
  - Commodity inventories;
  - Licensed carrier data;
  - Vehicle inventories;
  - Business directories;
  - Employment by freight activity;
  - Import and export statistics;
  - Mine output data;
  - Economic data;
  - Transportation infrastructure inventory and condition;
  - Pipeline volumes;
  - Traffic volumes;
  - Distribution warehouse truck traffic data;
  - Travel time, speed, and delay data;
  - Traffic bottlenecks;
  - Oversize and overweight permitting and routing data;
  - Safety data;
  - Fuel statistics; and
  - Emissions data and estimates.

- **Freight data models.** Freight data models refer to the set of data models needed to represent freight data characteristics and processes. Depending on the level of freight data architecture implementation selected, this part of the analysis will include selecting, developing, testing, and validating the corresponding data models needed. Typical data models might include the following:
  - Business process model,
  - Conceptual data model,
  - Logical data model,
  - Physical data model, and
  - Data dictionary.

  An alternative (or complement) to a data dictionary is a metadata document (*138*). Examples of metadata standards at the federal level are CSDGM (*106*), described earlier, and the Metadata Encoding and Transmission Standard (METS) (*139*). METS, which is maintained by the Library of Congress, is a standard for encoding descriptive, administrative, and structural metadata about library objects.

- **Freight data standards.** Freight data standards refer to documents that include specific requirements about structure, syntax, and content of freight data. The developer of the national freight data architecture will not be responsible for developing freight data standards. However, at a minimum, the data architecture developer should formulate recommendations for communication protocols with organizations responsible for developing relevant data standards and include "place holders" for data standard cross-references in the data architecture. Examples of data standards that pertain to freight information include the following:
  - Commodity and product classification standards
    - CPC
    - HMIS
    - HS
    - NAPCS
    - NMFC
    - NST 2007
    - PLU
    - SCTG
    - STCC
  - Industrial classification standards
    - ISIC
    - NAICS
    - SIC
    - SITC
  - Data exchange standards
    - ANSI ASC X12 standards
    - UN/EDIFACT standards
    - OASIS UBL standards
    - FIPS PUB 161-2

    – National ITS standards
    – FGDC-sponsored standards (including metadata)
    – Other standards
      ▪ ITDS SDS
      ▪ METS
      ▪ Vehicle classification standards.

- **User interface and supporting documentation.** User interface and supporting documentation refer to the system components and materials needed to present and disseminate information about the data architecture effectively. As the previous chapter shows, which confirms the findings of several reports, freight data are scattered across many systems, jurisdictions, and business processes. Having an information clearinghouse that describes these freight data sources and how they relate to the national freight data architecture will be critical to assist in the process of understanding and developing the data architecture. Depending on the data architecture implementation level selected, it will be necessary to develop interfaces and materials such as the following:

    – **Web-based information clearinghouse.** The purpose of the web-based information clearinghouse is to describe and explain the various components of the national freight data architecture interactively. Examples of systems that can be used as a reference to build this Website include the National ITS Architecture Website (*87*) and TranStats (*137*). Companion documentation to the Web-based system could include data models (see above), system design documents, and other standard reference materials.

    – **Outreach and training materials.** Examples of outreach and training materials include brochures, summaries, presentation files, instructor notes, and handouts to assist in the process of disseminating information about the national freight data architecture for use in venues, such as conferences, workshops, and courses.

Develop and Implement Protocols for Continuous Stakeholder Participation

Lack of proper stakeholder participation is one of major reasons for systems to fail. The developer of the national freight data architecture should develop channels of communication and mechanisms to ensure and document the participation of stakeholders at every step during the development of the data architecture. Specific requirements, in addition to those in connection with the implementation of the information clearinghouse and training materials, include the following:

- Articulate messages clearly,
- Provide clear, uniform guidance,
- Develop communication and marketing strategies,
- Identify and address buy-in and consensus issues,
- Identify and develop working relationships with data architecture champions,
- Develop a "showcase" to bring attention to the issue of freight data, and
- Develop a roadmap for collaboration between the public sector and the private sector for more effective data collection.

Conduct Data Gap Analysis

This report documented the results of a literature review, surveys, and follow-up interviews with a number of freight stakeholders, primarily planners, shippers, and motor carriers, to identify user and data needs. Targeted data gap analyses may be necessary to more precisely characterize user and data needs. This report identified (or further expanded on) a few areas where there are freight data gaps. Some gaps are related to limitations of current survey-based data collection programs. Other gaps are related to limitations in supply chain data processes or to the high degree of specialization of certain processes (e.g., shippers may have commodity data at a high level of disaggregation, but carriers do not need that level of commodity disaggregation to conduct business transactions).

Part of the process to identify data needs will be to develop a thorough understanding of the relationship between freight performance measures (many of which are still in the research and development phase) and the data needed to support those measures.

Conduct Data Disaggregation Need Analysis

Plenty of documents provide information about the limitations of current freight data collection programs, adding weight to the idea that current data sources are not sufficiently accurate or detailed. The data resolution issue is particularly critical because no statements are currently available that outline (1) the required data disaggregation and accuracy levels to address current and anticipated data collection needs from a technical and statistical perspective and (2) the corresponding impacts of those requirements on data collection costs and privacy requirements. Developing those statements is critical in order to identify data collection requirements.

Dimensions to freight data disaggregation could include areas such as commodity type disaggregation, geographic disaggregation, temporal disaggregation, financial data disaggregation, operating data disaggregation, and privacy requirements. Conducting the data disaggregation analysis is a significant effort. (Note that NCFRP Project 20 will address the issue of commodity flow geographic disaggregation).

Assume a Distributed Approach (as Opposed to a Centralized Approach) to Freight Data Repository Implementations

As previously mentioned, freight data are scattered across many systems, jurisdictions, and business processes. This practice is not likely to change any time soon. The availability of computerized processes that automate the collection and transmission of freight data will continue to increase—and the freight community should strive for continuous improvement and optimization of those processes. However, in the short to mid term, the chances for freight data exchange programs to succeed will depend greatly on the identification of integration points among disparate data systems; documentation of the location, characteristics, and limitations of those integration points; and the development of tools and processes (e.g., data conversion tools and survey tools) to facilitate data exchange.

Use a Systems Engineering Approach for Developing the National Freight Data Architecture

Systems engineering is an interdisciplinary approach to project development that focuses on the identification of user needs and required functionality early in the development process, documenting those requirements, and executing system verification and validation plans at different points during the development (*140*). Systems engineering is frequently used for the development of complex engineering and software projects, including many ITS implementations around

the country. Considering the complexity that characterizes freight data processes, it would be advisable to use a systems engineering approach for the development of the national freight data architecture (and any system implementation that could result from that effort). Key systems engineering principles that could apply to developing the national freight data architecture include the following (*140*):

- Keep an eye on the finish line,
- Stakeholder involvement is key,
- Define the problem before implementing the solution,
- Delay technology choices,
- Divide and conquer, and
- Connect the dots—maintain traceability.

Another tool in systems engineering that is frequently used, the "V" diagram (Figure 13), could also be used for developing the national freight data architecture (*140*). The V diagram shows the steps for developing systems, including the integration of validation activities throughout the process.

Use Standard Information Technology Tools and Procedures

In addition to the requirement to use a systems engineering approach is the requirement to use industry standard information technology tools and procedures (including data modeling, database, and software development tools) to develop the various components of the national freight data architecture. The choice of tools will need to take into consideration existing federal-level enterprise architecture requirements (*141*).

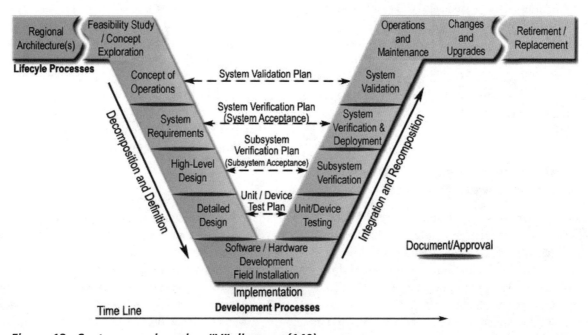

Figure 13. Systems engineering "V" diagram (140).

Develop and/or Use Standardized Terminology and Definitions for Each Data Architecture Component Developed

This requirement affects both information technology terms (such as architecture, data architecture, system, database, and framework) and freight transportation business process terms. This report includes a number of definitions the developer of the national freight data architecture should take into consideration. The developer also should note the various sources of freight-related terms and definitions that will need to be reconciled, particularly in the case of definition sources at the federal level. Examples of sources include the following:

- BTS's dictionary (142),
- CFS definitions (33),
- Economic Census definitions (143),
- Glossary from the Energy Information Administration (EIA) (144),
- FAF2 data dictionary (63), and
- IANA's glossary (145).

Implement Strong Privacy Protection Strategies

The national freight data architecture will need to comply with (and/or provide support to) the privacy provisions of the E-Government Act of 2002 (135, 136). Requirements in this act include conducting privacy impact assessments to document what information is to be collected, its purpose and intended use, information sharing practices and security measures, opportunities for consent, and whether a system of records is created following Privacy Act provisions. Beyond these legal requirements, the analysis will need to take into consideration confidentiality and anonymity requirements in connection with the participation of private-sector stakeholders (e.g., producers, shippers, and carriers) in data collection programs that result from the implementation of the national freight data architecture.

Establish Integration Points with Other Data Architectures and Standards

Although the main focus of the national freight data architecture will be freight planning (at least initially), it will need to provide support to, or ensure compatibility with, other data architectures. The national freight data architecture will also need to provide support to, or ensure compatibility with, applicable data standards. As previously mentioned, although the developer of the national freight data architecture will not be responsible for developing freight data standards, the data architecture developer should formulate recommendations for communication protocols with organizations responsible for developing relevant data standards and include "place holders" for data standard cross-references in the data architecture.

Challenges and Strategies

This section outlines some of the most relevant issues and challenges that might block the implementation of the national freight data architecture, as well as some candidate strategies for developing, adopting, and maintaining the data architecture.

Challenges and Potential Impediments to Successful Implementation

Technical Challenges

Technical challenges refer to issues (e.g., technological limitations, hardware and software incompatibilities, and standards incompatibilities) that might impede the successful implementation of the data architecture. Examples include the following:

- The national freight data architecture will be successful only if it meets the expectations of the freight community. This report laid out several implementation approaches for a national freight data architecture. Are the approaches appropriate? Will it be necessary to identify additional alternatives? What is the implementation horizon for each alternative?
- Data storage requirements may be enormous, even under a distributed, multi-agency data repository model. Will the key agencies responsible for managing the data have the necessary technical infrastructure and resources needed (e.g., servers, database system(s), and other applications) to undertake that task successfully?
- There may be tabulation errors and redundancies if more than one stakeholder needs to enter the same data. Ideally, data should be entered only once. However, is this scenario realistic with today's technologies, processes, and resources?
- Many motor carriers still rely on fax transmissions to move freight. Who will enter relevant data into a database to facilitate the collection of shipment data at the national level? Is it necessary for all motor carriers to be computerized? Is it necessary to collect data about all shipments?
- Upgrading computer systems at carriers and other freight stakeholders to support key elements of the national freight data architecture might take many years to implement, particularly if the objective is to obtain commodity flow data at finer levels of resolution. Financial considerations

aside, how feasible is it to deploy EFM and other similar initiatives throughout the entire supply chain? Even if computer systems are upgraded, one of the challenges would be how to address issues such as the common use of the generic freight-all-kinds freight classification to all shipments from a shipper regardless of freight commodity or type.

- Measurement units for commodities are different depending on the stakeholder. Further, commodity code classifications are different depending on the stakeholder. Is it possible to develop a comprehensive classification system that enables all crosswalks so that it could work for all stakeholders?
- Some data are not available in a timely fashion. For example, one agency reported that waiting for year-end reports did not allow the agency to find reporting irregularities early, forcing the agency to collect data on a quarterly basis. Feedback from the private sector indicates that the private sector does not make business decisions based on data they perceive to be old (e.g., CFS data). Under what circumstances is it possible to collect data more frequently than the current practice?
- Data quality control practices vary widely. How will different datasets be compared and integrated in a reliable way, even if datasets are not physically merged?
- There are substantial differences in terminology, data item definitions, and data implementations among freight data stakeholders. How feasible is it to identify integration points among disparate data systems; document the location, characteristics, and limitations of those integration points; and develop tools and processes (e.g., data conversion tools and survey tools) to facilitate data exchange?
- Not all data components may be necessary or should be considered high priority. Of course, whether a data component is important, urgent, or relevant is relative and depends on many factors. For example, a planner who is engaged in freight forecasting at the national level might not be interested in regional correlations between carrier operating data and transportation infrastructure characteristics and conditions. However, these data components are important to a regional planner who is developing recommendations for transportation improvement plans at the regional or state levels.
- Integrating data from shippers and carriers to characterize commodity movements properly may be challenging. Although both shippers and carriers are increasingly using EDI technologies, the type of data they collect is not necessarily the same. For example, a shipper might record commodities and O-D locations, but not routes. Similarly, a carrier might record routes and some generalized description of the commodities being transported, but not in a way that facilitates integration with shipper-produced data.

- Different stakeholders have different data confidentiality and data security concerns. Incorporating strong data security measures will be critical. However, there are technical challenges that would need to be addressed to make sure proper access is provided to users while complying with strong security standards.

Policy Challenges

The national freight data architecture might fail if required policies, both in the public and private sectors, fail or are not feasible. Examples of policy challenges include the following:

- Homeland security concerns may limit the dissemination of certain freight data. All import and export cargo is documented, yet the resulting data are not shared effectively among transportation planning agencies. Can interagency agreements be implemented to ensure that authorized personnel have access to relevant data in a timely manner, not just for hazardous materials as in the case of the HIP?
- Today, a number of private-sector associations, such as AAR and ATA, collect data from, or on behalf of, their members. What would be the impact of a national-level data collection effort on those initiatives?
- Anecdotal information suggests that collecting freight and company data is more difficult in the United States than in other industrialized countries due to differences in societal perceptions about the needs for, and benefits of, government regulation. However, freight and company data are widely exchanged daily (and voluntarily) by millions of trading partners in the private sector. Is it possible to reconcile these seemingly contradictory positions in a way that enables the collection of valuable data for freight transportation planning purposes? Is it possible to guarantee confidentiality and anonymity for data providers?

Economic and Financial Challenges

The national freight data architecture might fail if the perceived costs associated with its implementation exceed the benefits that stakeholders would receive. Examples of economic and financial challenges include the following:

- The cost of data collection, storage, and quality assurance will be enormous. Who will bear the cost of the implementation and how will the implementation be funded? Will users need to pay to access the data? If so, under what circumstances?
- Benefits from the implementation of the national freight data architecture might not materialize if the relationship between finer levels of data disaggregation and those

benefits has not been clearly established. What are the required levels of data disaggregation for different business processes?

- Access to data produced by private-sector data aggregators could be limited if the cost to acquire the data is prohibitive. Large organizations might be able to afford the data, but smaller organizations would not. What are the implications?
- Different stakeholders have different data confidentiality and data security concerns. Incorporating strong data security capabilities may be expensive, although necessary. Who will bear the cost for the implementation of those capabilities?

Stakeholder Buy-In and Consensus

The national freight data architecture might fail if there is no stakeholder buy-in or consensus about the potential benefits that could result from implementing the data architecture. Examples of related issues include the following:

- Stakeholders might be reluctant to participate if there is no clarity as to why they should participate or what kind of short-term and long-term benefits stakeholders could derive from participating. It will be critical to involve stakeholders early and often.
- Confidentiality clauses are often included in the contracts between supply chain trading partners. Participation in a national data collection program might compromise competitive advantages. Is it possible to implement strong privacy and confidentiality elements in the data architecture to satisfy the requirements of all the parties involved?
- Opposition could surface if there is a perception that data collected as part of a national freight data collection program could be used to validate projects of national significance at the expense of small or rural communities.
- Small carriers (e.g., independent owner-operators) might not have the ability to provide data about loads they move.
- If the number of stakeholder participants is too low, the resulting data might not be representative. It is important to ensure a minimum sample size to guarantee data reliability.
- Not all data standards may be adequate to support key elements of the national freight data architecture. What will be the challenges to obtain stakeholder support to upgrade those standards or to develop new standards that might be necessary?

Strategies for Successful Implementation

Strategies to ensure the successful implementation of the national freight data architecture include the following:

- Develop and compare candidate data architecture concepts. As previously mentioned, there are several possible implementation approaches for a national freight data architecture, some more ambitious and comprehensive than others. Completing the exercise of comparing data architecture concepts will enable stakeholders to develop a better understanding of the issues, which, in turn, will facilitate the development of a data architecture that meets stakeholder expectations.
- Identify business process and implementation level priorities and develop high-quality data architecture concepts and applications that address the needs of the highest priority items first. A successful initial implementation will increase the chances of success for future expansions of the data architecture.
- Identify data architecture leaders and champions. It is important to include representatives of the public sector (including federal, state, regional, and local levels) and the private sector (including producers, shippers, carriers, and third-party logistics and brokers).
- Engage the national freight data architecture champions early, identify major progress milestones, and maintain good communication channels with the various stakeholders during all phases of the development and implementation of the national freight transportation data architecture.
- Identify funding mechanisms for the implementation of the data architecture.
- Develop criteria for measuring the effectiveness in the implementation of the national freight data architecture.
- Tie the implementation of the national freight data architecture to the development of metrics or performance measures that could benefit the entire freight transportation community. Participation is likely to increase if the value proposition to stakeholders makes it clear how the data collected can help those stakeholders realize improvements in productivity (e.g., if the data collection program enables the identification of potential chokepoints in the supply chain).
- Accelerate the implementation of programs such as EFM and the freight performance measurement program. These programs are laying out the foundation for the collection of freight data at levels of disaggregation not possible before.
- Identify data needs at the finest disaggregation level and implement data collection and data storage plans at that level. This strategy will help stakeholders eliminate redundancy in data collection.
- Develop brochures, presentations, and other materials that explain the national freight data architecture, its scope, high-level components, and what it expects to accomplish. It will also be critical to deliver effective messages on how the national freight data architecture will assist stakeholders in the identification of strategies to address various freight-related issues ranging from data collection to analysis and reporting. Just as importantly, it will be critical to deliver messages that provide clear, concise answers to the

various challenges highlighted in the previous section. As previously mentioned, there is confusion in the freight transportation community about what the national freight data architecture initiative is. Presenting a clear message to the community will increase the chances of success.

- Articulate benefits of participation by the private sector and identify opportunities for public–private partnerships to make data accessible for transportation planning purposes in a cost-effective manner. Obtaining data from the private sector frequently has been challenging, which highlights the need to identify creative strategies to address this issue (e.g., by highlighting that existing freight data issues also affect the private sector, by contacting the right person at a sufficiently high administrative level for discussions about data access and sharing). A requirement for these partnerships is to ensure no competitive disruptions as a result of participation.

- Take into consideration lessons learned from the implementation and maintenance of existing freight-related systems and architectures. Chapter 2 included a detailed review of a sample of those systems, which included topics such as purpose, content, institutional arrangements; challenges and issues faced; strategies and methods for dealing with data integration issues; and adaptability.

CHAPTER 5

Conclusions and Recommendations

Introduction

The overarching theme behind NCFRP Project 12 was the need for accurate, comprehensive, timely freight transportation data at different levels, as well as the need for a holistic approach to freight transportation data. More specifically, NCFRP Project 12 was designed to identify specifications for a national freight data architecture that facilitates freight-related statistical and economic analyses; supports the decisionmaking process by public and private stakeholders at the national, state, regional, and local levels; and enables the acquisition and maintenance of critical data needed to identify freight-related transportation needs. Specific NCFRP Project 12 objectives included the following:

- Develop specifications for content and structure of a national freight data architecture that serves the needs of public and private decisionmakers at the national, state, regional, and local levels;
- Identify the value and challenges of the potential data architecture; and
- Specify institutional strategies to develop and maintain the data architecture.

The research team undertook the following activities to address these research needs:

- Completed a review of systems, databases, and architectures that might be used as a potential reference for the development of a national freight data architecture;
- Conducted surveys and follow-up interviews, interviews with subject matter experts, and a peer exchange with freight transportation stakeholders;
- Developed a formal definition for a national freight data architecture;
- Identified high-level categories of data architecture components;
- Identified potential implementation approaches;

- Developed a list of specifications for a national freight data architecture; and
- Identified challenges and strategies related to the implementation of a national freight data architecture.

It is worth noting that the purpose of NCFRP Project 12 was to develop requirements and specifications for a national freight data architecture, not to develop the data architecture (which would be a logical next step after identifying those requirements and specifications).

Data Sources, Systems, and Architectures

A variety of listings, links, and summaries of systems, databases, architectures, and other related documents that pertain to freight transportation data are available in the literature. Although there is a wealth of sources of information that pertain to freight transportation, a comprehensive catalog of freight-related data sources at different geographic levels (including national, state, regional, and local levels) does not exist. As a reference, the research team conducted a review of a sample of freight-related data sources at the national level to complement or otherwise extend existing listings. Previously shown Table 1 provides a list of freight data sources reviewed in this report. Appendix A of the contractor's final report (available on the project web page) includes an augmented version of this table, with data sources expanded at the dataset level. This appendix also includes a detailed description of each data source.

The list of freight data sources in Table 1 is obviously not comprehensive. For example, it does not reference datasets that state, regional, and local entities need to collect to supplement or augment national-level datasets. Although the list in Table 1 does not include all of the potential data sources that deal with freight transportation, it is useful because it provides a sample of the typical national-level data sources that would need to be included in a national freight data architecture. A few systems and architectures in Table 1 were of particular interest because of the lessons that could be derived from the processes that led to their development. The analysis included topics such as purpose, content, institutional arrangements used for developing and maintaining the system or architecture; challenges and issues faced in creating and maintaining the architecture or system; strategies and methods for dealing with data integration issues; and adaptability to serve evolving purposes and data sources.

Online Surveys, Interviews, and Peer Exchange

The research team conducted a planner and analyst survey, a shipper survey, and a motor carrier survey (as well as follow-up interviews) to gather information about freight data uses and needs. The research team also conducted interviews with subject matter experts to address specific items of interest to the research. The purpose of the planner and analyst survey was to gather information from government planners, analysts, and other similar freight-related stakeholders. The invitation to participate in the survey included groups such as AASHTO committees, TRB committees, and AMPO. Respondents were involved in all modes of transportation, including air, rail, truck, pipelines, and water. Not surprisingly (given that respondents were typically public-sector planners), most respondents indicated that they use freight data to support the production of public-sector transportation planning documents. However, respondents also reported using data for various other freight-related applications, adding weight to the notion that the national freight data architecture should support various freight-related processes. Respondents reported using and/or needing data at various levels of geographic coverage and resolution. The feedback on unmet data needs complement similar findings in the literature.

The purpose of the shipper survey was to gather general information from the shipper community regarding freight data uses and needs, as well as willingness to share data with other freight-related stakeholders. The survey included representatives of companies of various sizes, including third-party logistics, freight forwarders, manufacturers, retailers, and suppliers. The shipper industry collects large amounts of data. Many shippers and logistics service providers transmit data electronically using EDI technologies. These stakeholders use EDI regularly for load tendering, tracking, and billing purposes. However, accessing data from shippers and logistics service providers for transportation planning applications (beyond aggregated data from commercial data providers and national survey campaigns such as CFS) is not necessarily straightforward. For example, although a data record might

characterize a commodity as well as origin and destination locations, the route data component may be missing.

In addition, the shipper stakeholders interviewed indicated they could not comment on their companies' ability or willingness to share data for freight transportation planning purposes (particularly on a load-by-load basis, given its proprietary and confidential nature). Subsequent feedback obtained at the peer exchange (see below) highlighted a number of strategies to address this issue, including initiating discussions about data sharing at a sufficiently high administrative level—since low-ranking personnel might know the data, but frequently do not have the authority or permission to discuss data sharing options. Involving trade associations rather than individual firms also might be beneficial. A business model also might emerge in which data providers would forward sample data to a designated agency on a predetermined schedule for developing a commodity flow database at the national level. The data would be stripped of certain identifiers to address privacy and confidentiality concerns. Although the data would not be available for free (since filtering, forwarding, storing, and processing the data would involve real costs), it is anticipated that the cost of collecting the data would be a fraction of the cost to conduct normal surveys.

The purpose of the motor carrier survey was to gather information from the motor carrier community about freight data uses and needs, as well as willingness to share data with external freight-related stakeholders. Survey respondents represented all major sectors of the motor carrier industry, including TL, LTL, and specialized. As in the case of shippers, motor carriers expressed reservations about sharing proprietary and confidential data. In particular, their reservations were related to the need to develop mechanisms to protect proprietary and confidential information and to maintain the anonymity of carriers and customers. In general, carriers would need to know in advance the specific uses of the data and, in return, would expect information in the form of industry benchmarking metrics. It is worth noting that developing metrics of interest to the private sector is part of the scope of work of NCFRP Project 3, "Performance Measures for Freight Transportation."

In practice, the type and amount of data provided by, or available through, carriers varies considerably, depending on factors such as carrier size, geographic locations, activity focus, and type of cargo transported. Carriers handle large amounts of disaggregated data during the course of their business operations. Increasingly, carriers use EDI standards and applications. However, most of this information is confidential and limited to the direct exchange of data between trading partners. In addition, the amount of shipment information detail varies according to the type of carrier. For example, TL carriers, who tend to bill customers on a per-mile basis or by using a flat rate, rarely collect detailed commodity data. In addition, TL carriers are less likely to collect data on tonnage hauled or tare-level data, also attributable to industry-accepted billing practices. By comparison, LTL carriers typically bill customers using a rate structure based on shipment weight, origin, destination, and freight classification. However, there is anecdotal evidence that LTL carriers tend to favor a freight-all-kinds rating structure that assigns a general freight classification to all shipments from a shipper regardless of freight commodity or type. As opposed to TL carriers, LTL carriers are more likely to track total tonnage.

In conjunction with the 2009 North American Freight Flows Conference in Irvine, CA, the research team organized a peer exchange to discuss preliminary research findings; request feedback; and facilitate a dialogue on implementation strategies to develop, adopt, and maintain a national freight data architecture. Participants included representatives of federal, state, regional, university, and private-sector agencies. To encourage participation and discussion, attendees received background materials such as relevant research topic summaries and breakout group agendas and discussion objectives. Feedback from peer exchange participants included recommendations for changes to initial research findings as well as a list of issues, challenges, and strategies to consider during the implementation of the national freight data architecture.

National Freight Data Architecture Definition

Taking into consideration the results of the literature review, as well as feedback from surveys, follow-up interviews, and the peer exchange, the research team developed the following generic definition for a national freight data architecture:

> The national freight data architecture is the manner in which data elements are organized and integrated for freight transportation-related applications or business processes. The data architecture includes the necessary set of tools that describe related functions or roles, components where those roles reside or apply, and data flows that connect roles and components at different domain and aggregation levels.

Depending on the specific level of implementation chosen for the data architecture, this generic definition could be fine-tuned as follows:

- **Single-application approach.** In this case, the national freight data architecture would become the manner in which data elements are organized and integrated for *a specific* freight application or business process at the national level (e.g., commodity flows).
- **Intermediate approaches (depending on the number of applications).** In this case, the national freight data architecture would become the manner in which data elements are organized and integrated for *a specific set* of applications at

the national, state, regional, and local levels. A large number of intermediate approaches is possible, depending on the business processes and geographic levels involved. For example, an intermediate implementation approach could include commodity flows at the national, state, and regional levels. Another, more encompassing, intermediate implementation approach could include commodity flows, safety, and pavement impacts at the national, state, regional, and local levels.

- **Holistic, all-encompassing approach.** In this case, the national freight data architecture would become the manner in which data elements are organized and integrated for *all* freight transportation-related applications or business processes at the national, state, regional, and local levels.

For any of these implementation options, the data architecture would include the necessary set of tools that describe related functions or roles, components where those roles reside or apply, and data flows that connect roles and components.

National Freight Data Architecture Value

From the documentation and information gathered during the research, the research team identified the following list of benefits that, together, provide a statement of value for the national freight data architecture:

- Better understanding of the different business processes that affect freight transportation at different levels of coverage and resolution;
- Better understanding of the supply chain, which should help transportation planners to identify strategies for improving freight transportation infrastructure;
- Better understanding of the role that different public-sector and private-sector stakeholders play on freight transportation;
- Better understanding of the need for standards to assist in data exchange;
- Systematic, coordinated development of reference datasets (e.g., comprehensive commodity code crosswalk tables);
- Systematic inventory of freight transportation data sources;
- Systematic inventory of user and data needs that are prerequisites for the development of freight data management systems;
- Use as a reference for the identification of locations where there may be freight data redundancy and inefficiencies;
- Use as a reference for requesting funding allocations in the public and private sectors; and
- Use as a reference for the development of outreach, professional development, and training materials.

In practice, the value of the national freight data architecture is also a function of the costs associated with its implementation. Quantifiable data about expected benefits and costs are currently not available (benefit-cost analyses need to occur both at the beginning and at different phases of implementation of the national freight data architecture). However, it is clear from the documentation and information gathered during the research that the "do-nothing" alternative (i.e., not implementing the national freight data architecture) is costly, ineffective, and, unsustainable. Therefore, the research team's recommendation is to pursue the national freight data architecture following a scalable implementation path in which the national freight data architecture starts with one application at one or two levels of decisionmaking and then adds applications and levels of decisionmaking as needed or according to a predetermined implementation plan until, eventually, reaching the maximum net value.

National Freight Data Architecture Components

The research team identified the following categories of components to include in the national freight data architecture:

- Physical transportation components,
- Cargo or freight,
- Freight functions or roles,
- Business processes,
- Data sources,
- Freight-related data,
- Freight data models,
- Freight data standards, and
- User interface and supporting documentation.

Figure 10 (shown previously) presents a high-level modular conceptualization and list of different categories of components. The diagram recognizes the scalable nature of the national freight data architecture and enables the production of a variety of diagram versions (as well as tabular representations) depending on what implementation level to pursue. For example, for a single-application data architecture that only focuses on commodity flows at the national level, it may not be necessary to depict (at least not in detail) other freight functions and business processes. Similarly, not all data standards would need to be considered, and the requirements for user interfaces to support that data architecture would be relatively minor.

The diagram in Figure 10 is only one example of potentially many different types of diagrams that can be used to depict interactions among freight transportation components. An example of a different type of diagram previously shown is Figure 12, which presents a high-level conceptual model that focuses on relationships between different individual data architecture components for specific business processes.

National Freight Data Architecture Recommendations and Specifications

In addition to the list of categories and components, the research team put together a list of recommendations for the development and implementation of the national freight data architecture. For convenience, the recommendations are written in the form of specifications to guide and monitor the implementation of the data architecture.

Chapter 4 provides a detailed discussion of each specification item. For compactness, only the title of each specification is listed here:

- Adopt a definition for the national freight data architecture that is generic, scalable, and is understood and accepted by the freight transportation community (see proposed definition above);
- Compare candidate data architecture implementation concepts;
- Develop implementation plan for national freight data architecture components;
- Develop lists of components to include in the national freight data architecture;
- Develop and implement protocols for continuous stakeholder participation;
- Conduct data gap analysis;
- Conduct data disaggregation need analysis;
- Assume a distributed approach (as opposed to a centralized approach) to freight data repository implementations;
- Use a systems engineering approach for developing the national freight data architecture;
- Use standard information technology tools and procedures;
- Develop and/or use standardized terminology and definitions for each data architecture component developed;
- Implement strong privacy protection strategies; and
- Establish integration points with other data architectures and standards.

Challenges and Strategies

The research team identified relevant issues and challenges that might block the implementation of the national freight data architecture, as well as candidate strategies for developing, adopting, and maintaining the data architecture. The challenges were in the following categories: technical challenges, policy challenges, economic and financial challenges, and stakeholder buy-in and consensus. Chapter 4 provides a detailed description of each challenge. Only a summarized list of challenges is provided here.

- **Technical challenges.** Technical challenges refer to issues (e.g., technological limitations, hardware and software incompatibilities, and standards incompatibilities) that might impede the successful implementation of the data architecture. Examples include the following:
  - Feasibility of different implementation approaches;
  - Data storage requirements;
  - Feasibility of updated data entry protocols to eliminate data redundancies and support standardized data entry procedures;
  - Conversion of commodity code classifications;
  - Data life cycle and usefulness to support the decision-making process by public and private stakeholders;
  - Variability in data quality control practices, which affect data accuracy, completeness, and timeliness;
  - Differences in terminology, data item definitions, and data implementations among freight data stakeholders;
  - Prioritization of data architecture components;
  - Integration between shipper and carrier data to characterize commodity movements properly; and
  - Data confidentiality and security concerns.
- **Policy challenges.** The national freight data architecture might fail if required policies, both in the public and private sectors, fail or are not feasible. Examples of policy challenges include the following:
  - Homeland security concerns, which might limit the dissemination of certain freight-related data;
  - Impact on current private-sector data collection initiatives; and
  - Competitive and proprietary (privacy) concerns with the concept of public-sector agencies having access to private-sector data.
- **Economic and financial challenges.** The national freight data architecture might fail if the perceived costs associated with its implementation exceed the benefits that stakeholders would receive. Examples of economic and financial challenges include the following:
  - Cost of data collection, storage, and quality assurance;
  - Benefits and costs related to data disaggregation requirements for different business processes;
  - Data life cycle and usefulness to support the decision-making process by public and private stakeholders;
  - Cost to acquire private-sector data; and
  - Cost to implement robust data confidentiality and data security measures.
- **Stakeholder buy-in and consensus.** The national freight data architecture might fail if there is no stakeholder buy-in or consensus about the potential benefits that could result from implementing the data architecture. Examples of related issues include the following:
  - Reluctance of stakeholders to participate if there is no clarity regarding justification and anticipated benefits;
  - Confidentiality clauses in supply chain contracts, which might impede data sharing for transportation planning purposes;
  - Perception that data collected as part of a national freight data collection program could validate projects of national significance at the expense of small or rural communities;
  - Ability of small carriers to provide data about loads they move;
  - Risk of low stakeholder participation, which could decrease data reliability; and
  - Adequacy of data standards.

Strategies to ensure a successful implementation of the national freight data architecture include the following:

- Implementation levels
  - Develop and compare candidate data architecture concepts,
  - Identify business process and implementation level priorities,
  - Develop high-quality data architecture concepts and applications that address the needs of the highest priority items first, and
  - Identify data needs at the finest disaggregation level and implement data collection and data storage plans at that level.
- Relationships with leaders, champions, and stakeholders
  - Identify data architecture leaders and champions;
  - Engage the national freight data architecture champions early;
  - Maintain good communication channels with the various stakeholders during all phases of the development and implementation of the national freight transportation data architecture;
  - Identify funding mechanisms for the implementation of the data architecture;
  - Develop brochures, presentations, and other materials that explain the national freight data architecture, its scope, high-level components, and what it expects to accomplish;
  - Deliver effective messages on how the national freight data architecture will assist stakeholders in the identification of strategies to address a variety of freight-related issues ranging from data collection to analysis and reporting;
  - Deliver messages that provide clear, concise answers to the various challenges highlighted in the previous section;
  - Articulate benefits of participation by the private sector; and
  - Identify opportunities for partnerships with the private sector (e.g., through public–private partnerships) to make

data accessible for transportation planning purposes in a cost-effective manner.

- Performance measures and effectiveness
  - Develop criteria for measuring the effectiveness in the implementation of the national freight data architecture,
  - Identify major progress milestones,
  - Tie the implementation of the national freight data architecture to the development of metrics or performance measures that could benefit the entire freight transportation community, and
  - Accelerate the implementation of programs such as EFM and the freight performance measurement program.
- Lessons learned from the implementation and maintenance of existing freight-related systems and architectures (see Chapter 2 for detailed information about these systems and architectures)
  - Develop systems that are relevant to stakeholders, include adequate stakeholder participation, and provide incentives to encourage participation—particularly in the case of state and local entities;
  - Clearly define expected outcomes and development and coordination plan;
  - Articulate programs well; provide clear, uniform guidance; and provide good documentation;
  - Develop applications that rely on widely used data standards;
  - Develop and compare candidate architecture concepts;
  - Consider federal legislation to support and develop the program;
  - Develop tools to measure benefits and costs early;
  - Integrate archived data needs into frameworks and architectures early and develop data programs that use industry standards;
  - Implement interagency data exchange programs with centralized data coordination;
  - Use available data sources and develop long-term plans while keeping systems flexible to respond to changes and new data sources;
  - Schedule major and regular revisions effectively while avoiding scope creep;
  - Develop systems that are consistent with input data limitations;
  - Develop applications with backward compatibility;
  - Evaluate data disaggregation level requirements to ensure statistical significance;
  - Provide adequate resources for data collection, fully understand the implications of small sample sizes, and continue to involve the U.S. Census Bureau for the use of survey instruments;
  - Emphasize data access, quality, reliability, confidentiality, and integrity;
  - Participate in the standards development process;
  - Create crosswalks to ensure compatibility of survey data internally over time and externally across other datasets;
  - Involve stakeholders early and often through a variety of mechanisms and technologies; and
  - Develop and implement professional capacity and training programs early.

One of the strategies for implementation mentioned above is to develop and compare candidate data architecture concepts. Peer exchange participants highlighted that implementing a comprehensive data architecture at once with no testing of options prior to making a decision about the correct approach would be too risky. Participants also favored the concept of developing and comparing several alternative approaches.

A recommendation from peer exchange participants was to use NCFRP as an avenue for funding the development of alternative data architecture concepts. Participants indicated the request for proposals should outline clear objectives, while leaving the definition of approaches to the research team(s) selected. An idea discussed was to develop the data architecture around scenarios or themes, such as business areas or processes, levels of government, or economic activity. Activities in connection with each scenario or theme would include structuring a competition for research teams (each of which would include a university partner, a private-sector partner, and a government-level partner) to develop and test competing data architecture concepts, making sure to include multimodal components in the scenarios and tests, and conduct a follow-up evaluation.

References

1. Kim, Sharon, Sedor, Joanne, and Schmitt, Rolf. *Freight Facts and Figures 2007*. Publication FHWA-HOP-08-004. Federal Highway Administration, Office of Freight Management and Operations, U.S. Department of Transportation, Washington D.C., 2007.

2. *Transportation Statistics Beyond ISTEA: Critical Gaps and Strategic Responses*. Publication BTS98-A-01. Bureau of Transportation Statistics, U.S. Department of Transportation, Washington D.C., 1998.

3. *Freight Transportation*. National Policy and Strategies Can Help Improve Freight Mobility. Report GAO-08-287, United States Government Accountability Office, Washington, D.C., January 2008. http://www.gao.gov/new.items/d08287.pdf. Accessed September 14, 2009.

4. *Special Report 276: A Concept for a National Freight Data Program*. Transportation Research Board, National Research Council, Washington, D.C., 2003.

5. Conference on Data Needs in the Changing World of Logistics and Freight Transportation. Saratoga Springs, New York, 2001. https://www.nysdot.gov/divisions/policy-and-strategy/darb/dai-unit/ttss/repository/synthesis.pdf. Accessed September 10, 2009.

6. M. Bronzini and S. Singuluri. *Scoping Study for a Freight Data Exchange Network*. Project 8-36, Task 79, National Cooperative Highway Research Program, Transportation Research Board, Washington, D.C., June 2009.

7. E. Wittwer, T. Adams, T. Gordon, J. Gupta, P. Lindquist, M. Vonderembse, K. Kawamura, and S. McNeil. *Upper Midwest Freight Corridor Study*. Report FHWA/OH 2005-01-20252B, Midwest Regional University Transportation Center, Madison, Wisconsin, March 2005. http://midwestfreightdata.utoledo.edu/style/doc/umfcs_final report_p1.pdf. Accessed December 11, 2009.

8. Framework for a National Freight Policy. U.S. Department of Transportation, Washington, D.C., undated. http://www.freight.dot.gov/freight_framework/index.cfm. Accessed May 8, 2009.

9. Freight Professional Development—Federal Sources of Freight Data. Office of Freight Management and Operations, Federal Highway Administration, Washington, D.C., October 2004. http://ops.fhwa.dot.gov/freight/fpd/Docs/freightdata/freightdata.htm. Accessed May 11, 2009.

10. Data Sources. Office of Freight Management and Operations, Federal Highway Administration, Washington, D.C., December 2008. http://www.ops.fhwa.dot.gov/freight/freight_analysis/data_sources.htm. Accessed May 11, 2009.

11. D. Beagan, M. Fischer, and A. Kuppam. *Quick Response Freight Manual II*. Report FHWA-HOP-08-010, Federal Highway Administration, Washington, D.C., September 2007. http://ops.fhwa.dot.gov/freight/publications/qrfm2/index.htm. Accessed May 11, 2009.

12. S. Maccalous and A. Phillips. *Directory of Transportation Data Sources, 1996*. Report DOT-VNTSC-BTS-96-3, Bureau of Transportation Statistics, U.S. Department of Transportation, Washington, D.C., June 1996.

13. F. Southworth. *A Preliminary Roadmap for the American Freight Data Program (DRAFT)*. Bureau of Transportation Statistics, U.S. Department of Transportation, Washington, D.C., December 2004. http://onlinepubs.trb.org/onlinepubs/archive/committees/data section/AM-AmericanFreight.pdf. Accessed September 11, 2009.

14. A. Mani and J. Prozzi. *State-of-the-Practice in Freight Data: A Review of Available Freight Data in the U.S.* Product 0-4713-P2. Texas Department of Transportation, Austin, Texas, February 2004.

15. ACE: Modernization Information Systems. U.S. Customs and Border Protection, U.S. Department of Homeland Security, Washington, D.C., undated. http://www.cbp.gov/xp/cgov/trade/automated/modernization/. Accessed May 11, 2009.

16. Information Technology. Customs Automated Commercial Environment Program Progressing, but Need for Management Improvements Continues. Report GAO-05-267. U.S. Government Accountability Office, Washington, D.C., March 2005. http://www.gao.gov/new.items/d05267.pdf. Accessed September 5, 2009.

17. International Trade Data System, undated. http://www.itds.gov/. Accessed May 11, 2009.

18. Public Law 106-554, December 21, 2000. http://www.gpoaccess.gov/plaws/106publ.html. Accessed September 14, 2009.

19. Audit of the Automated Commercial Environment Secure Data Portal: Management Controls Needed Improvement. Report OIG-04-35, Office of the Inspector General, Department of Homeland Security, Washington, D.C., September 2004. http://www.dhs.gov/xoig/assets/mgmtrpts/OIG_04-35_Sep04.pdf. Accessed September 14, 2009.

20. Topic: ACE 101. U.S. Customs and Border Protection, U.S. Department of Homeland Security, Washington, D.C., April 2009. http://www.cbp.gov/linkhandler/cgov/trade/automated/modernization/ace/ace101.ctt/ace101.pdf. Accessed September 7, 2009.

21. S. Shackerlford, J. Short, and D. Murray. *Assessing the Impact of the ACE Truck E-Manifest System on Trucking Operations*. American Transportation Research Institute, U.S. Customs and Border Protection, U.S. Department of Homeland Security, Washington, D.C., March 2007.

22. ACE Behind-the-Scenes. U.S. Customs and Border Protection, U.S. Department of Homeland Security, Washington, D.C., May 2008. http://www.cbp.gov/xp/cgov/trade/automated/moderniza tion/whats_new/whats_new_ace_archives/2008/april_may08_ archive/ace_behind_scenes.xml. Accessed September 7, 2009.

23. Report to Congress on the International Trade Data Systems (ITDS), November 2007.

24. International Freight Data System (IFDS) Privacy Impact Statement. Research and Innovative Technology Administration, Washington, D.C., February 2009. http://www.dot.gov/pia/rita_ifds.htm. Accessed May 11, 2009.

25. Industry Data > Economic Data: Waybill. Surface Transportation Board, U.S. Department of Transportation, Washington, D.C., undated. http://www.stb.dot.gov/stb/industry/econ_waybill.html. Accessed May 27, 2009.

26. 49 CFR 1241-1248. Reports. http://ecfr.gpoaccess.gov/cgi/t/text/ text-idx?sid=cdd81aef24b8005ebc55acb16dfd8a3f&c=ecfr&tpl=/ ecfrbrowse/Title49/49cfrv9_02.tpl. Accessed May 28, 2009.

27. Reference Guide for the 2007 Surface Transportation Board Carload Waybill Sample. Surface Transportation Board, U.S. Department of Transportation, Washington, D.C., July 2008. http://www. stb.dot.gov/stb/docs/Waybill/2007%20STB%20Waybill%20Reference%20Guide.pdf. Accessed August 31, 2009.

28. Railroad Service in United States, 2007. Association of American Railroads, undated. http://www.aar.org/~/media/AAR/2007_RailroadsAndStates/US%20summary.ashx. Accessed September 3, 2009.

29. Industry Data > Economic Data: Financial & Statistical Reports. Surface Transportation Board, U.S. Department of Transportation, Washington, D.C., undated. http://www.stb.dot.gov/stb/industry/ econ_reports.html. Accessed May 27, 2009.

30. 49 CFR 225. Railroad Accidents/Incidents: Reports Classification and Investigation. http://ecfr.gpoaccess.gov/cgi/t/text/text-idx?c= ecfr&sid=74ae91403a273c85911a65bc6f339baf&rgn=div5&view= text&node=49:4.1.1.1.20&idno=49. Accessed May 29, 2009.

31. Rail Cost Adjustment Factor. American Association of Railroads, undated. http://www.aar.org/~/media/AAR/RailCostIndexes/ Index_RCAFDescription.ashx. Accessed September 5, 2009.

32. Industry Data>Economic Data: RCAF. Surface Transportation Board, U.S. Department of Transportation, Washington, D.C., undated. http://www.stb.dot.gov/stb/industry/rcaf.html. Accessed September 3, 2009.

33. Commodity Flow Survey. Bureau of Transportation Statistics, Research and Innovative Technology Administration, Washington, D.C., undated. http://www.bts.gov/programs/commodity_ flow_survey/. Accessed May 11, 2009.

34. Commodity Flow Survey. Frequently Asked Questions. Bureau of Transportation Statistics, Research and Innovative Technology Administration, Washington, D.C., undated. http://www.bts.gov/ help/commodity_flow_survey.html. Accessed May 11, 2009.

35. *Measuring Personal Travel and Goods Movement: A Review of the Bureau of Transportation Statistics' Surveys.* Special Report 277. Transportation Research Board, National Research Council, Washington, D.C., 2003. http://trb.org/publications/sr/sr277.pdf. Accessed September 6, 2009.

36. Freight in America: A New National Picture. Bureau of Transportation Statistics, Research and Innovative Technology Administration, U.S. Department of Transportation, Washington, D.C., January 2006. http://www.bts.gov/publications/freight_in_america/ pdf/entire.pdf. Accessed September 6, 2009.

37. Commodity Flow Survey Conference. E-C088. Transportation Research Circular, Transportation Research Board, Washington, D.C., January 2006. http://www.trb.org/publications/circulars/ ec088.pdf. Accessed May 11, 2009.

38. P. Scheinberg. *Surface Transportation: Improvements in the Bureau of Transportation Statistics' Commodity Flow Survey.* Report GAO/ RCED-98-90R. United States General Accounting Office, Washington, D.C., February 1998. http://archive.gao.gov/paprpdf2/159984. pdf. Accessed September 6, 2009.

39. *Special Report 234: Data for Decisions: Requirements for National Transportation Policy Making.* Transportation Research Board, National Research Council, Washington, D.C., 1992.

40. H. Shin, and L. Aultman-Hall. Development of Nation-Wide Freight Analysis Zones. 86th Annual Meeting, Transportation Research Board, Washington, D.C., January 2007.

41. ASC X12. Accredited Standards Committee X12, Data Interchange Standards Association, Falls Church, Virginia, 2009. http://www. x12.org/. Accessed August 31, 2009.

42. UN/EDIFACT-ISO9735. United Nations Centre for Trade Facilitation and Electronics Business, May 2009. http://www.unece. org/cefact/. Accessed May 28, 2009.

43. ubl xml.org. Undated. http://ubl.xml.org/. Accessed December 10, 2009.

44. Electronic Data Interchange (EDI). Federal Information Processing Standards Publication 161-2, National Institute of Standards and Technology, Gaithersburg, Maryland, April 29, 1996. http://www. itl.nist.gov/fipspubs/fip161-2.htm. Accessed May 11, 2009.

45. 45 CFR 160 and 162. Administrative Data Standards and Related Requirements. http://ecfr.gpoaccess.gov/cgi/t/text/text-idx?sid= f3136244f528a0f781bef116d8e71a77&c=ecfr&tpl=/ecfrbrowse/ Title45/45cfrv1_02.tpl. Accessed December 7, 2009.

46. The National Motor Freight Classification. National Motor Freight Traffic Association, Alexandria, Virginia, undated. http:// www.nmfta.org/Pages/Nmfc.aspx. Accessed May 11, 2009.

47. Available Classifications. United Nations, New York, New York, undated. http://unstats.un.org/unsd/cr/registry/regct.asp?Lg=1. Accessed September 4, 2009.

48. NST 2007. United Nations Economic Commission for Europe. ECE/TRANS/WP.6/155/Add.1, June 2008. http://www.unece.org/ trans/main/wp6/transstatwp6nst.html. Accessed May 7, 2010.

49. Nomenclature. World Customs Organization, Brussels, Belgium, undated. http://www.wcoomd.org/home_wco_topics_hsoverview boxes.htm. Accessed September 4, 2009.

50. Tariff Information Center. United States International Trade Commission, Washington, D.C., 2006. http://www.usitc.gov/tata/ hts/index.htm. Accessed May 11, 2009.

51. 49 USC 13703. Certain collective activities; exemption from antitrust laws. http://uscode.house.gov/uscode-cgi/fastweb.exe?get doc+uscview+t49t50+346+0++%28%29%20%20AND%20%28% 2849%29%20ADJ%20USC%29%3ACITE%20AND%20%28USC %20w%2F10%20%2813703%29%29%3ACITE%20%20%20%20 %20%20%20%20%20. Accessed May 11, 2009.

52. Participation/Membership. National Motor Freight Traffic Association, Alexandria, Virginia, undated. http://www.nmfta.org/ Pages/MembershipDescription.aspx. Accessed May 11, 2009.

53. North American Product Classification System. U.S. Census Bureau, Washington, D.C., July 2007. http://www.census.gov/eos/ www/napcs/napcs.htm. Accessed May 11, 2009.

54. Produce PLU. A User's Guide—2006. International Federation for Produce Standards, Newark, Delaware, 2006. http://www. plucodes.com/docs/IFPS-plu_codes_users_guide.pdf. Accessed May 29, 2009.

55. Standard Classification of Transported Goods (SCTG) Codes. Bureau of Transportation Statistics, Research and Innovative

Technology Administration, Washington, D.C., undated. http://www.bts.gov/programs/commodity_flow_survey/methods_and_limitations/commodity_classification_in_1997/hierarchical_features.html. Accessed September 4, 2009.

56. *Standard Transportation Commodity Code. History and Background.* STCC—Standard Transportation Commodity Code File, Railinc, Cary, North Carolina, September 1996. https://community.railinc.com/products/irf/STCC%20%20Standard%20Transportation%20Commodity%20Code%20File/Forms/AllItems.aspx. Accessed May 11, 2009.

57. FAF2 Technical Documentation. Office of Freight Management and Operations, Federal Highway Administration, Washington, D.C., 2008. http://ops.fhwa.dot.gov/freight/freight_analysis/faf/faf2_tech_document.htm. Accessed May 11, 2009.

58. NAICS Association, Rockaway, New Jersey, 2009. http://www.naics.com. Accessed September 5, 2009.

59. SIC Division Structure. Occupational Safety and Health Administration, United States Department of Labor, Washington, D.C., undated. http://www.osha.gov/pls/imis/sic_manual.html. Accessed September 4, 2009.

60. Concordances. U.S. Census Bureau, Washington, D.C., January 2004. http://www.census.gov/epcd/naics/concordances/index.html. Accessed September 5, 2009.

61. Freight Analysis Framework (FAF). Office of Freight Management and Operations, Federal Highway Administration, Washington, D.C., 2009. http://ops.fhwa.dot.gov/freight/freight_analysis/faf/. Accessed May 11, 2009.

62. D. Beagan, M. Fischer, and A. Kuppam. *Quick Response Freight Analysis II.* Report FHWA-HOP-08-010, Office of Freight Management and Operations, Federal Highway Administration, Washington, D.C., 2009. http://ops.fhwa.dot.gov/freight/publications/qrfm2/index.htm. Accessed September 5, 2009.

63. Freight Analysis Framework (FAF), Version 2.2, User Guide. Office of Freight Management and Operations, Federal Highway Administration, Washington, D.C., 2009. http://ops.fhwa.dot.gov/freight/freight_analysis/faf/faf2_tech_document.htm. Accessed May 11, 2009.

64. R. Schmitt. Initial Thoughts on FAF2 Experience and FAF3 Design. Office of Freight Management and Operations, Federal Highway Administration, Washington, D.C., November 2008. http://www.ops.fhwa.dot.gov/freight/freight_analysis/faf/faf2faf3thoughtsnov8.htm. Accessed September 5, 2009.

65. *Freight Analysis Framework: Issues and Plans.* Office of Freight Management and Operations, Federal Highway Administration, Washington, D.C., September 2004.

66. Highway Performance Monitoring System. Federal Highway Administration, Washington, D.C., August 2008. http://www.fhwa.dot.gov/policy/ohpi/hpms/index.cfm. Accessed May 11, 2009.

67. *Highway Performance Monitoring System Field Manual for the Continuing Analytical and Statistical Database.* Report OMB 21250028, Federal Highway Administration, Washington, D.C., May 2005. http://www.fhwa.dot.gov/ohim/hpmsmanl/hpms.cfm. Accessed May 11, 2009.

68. *HPMS Reassessment 2010+ Final Report.* Office of Highway Policy Information, Federal Highway Administration, U.S. Department of Transportation, Washington, D.C., September 2008. http://knowledge.fhwa.dot.gov/cops/hcx.nsf/All+Documents/99E6D7EF08ED5675852574C20063D0A3/$FILE/HPMS%20Reassessment%20Final%20Report%209-12-08.pdf. Accessed August 31, 2009.

69. Intermodal Surface Transportation Efficiency Act of 1991. Public Law 102-240, December 18, 1991.

70. Transportation Equity Act for the 21st Century. Public Law 105-178, June 9, 1998. http://www.gpoaccess.gov/plaws/105publ.html. Accessed August 28, 2009.

71. Safe, Accountable, Flexible, Efficient Transportation Equity Act: A Legacy for Users. Public Law 109-59, August 10, 2005. http://www.gpoaccess.gov/plaws/109publ.html. Accessed August 28, 2009.

72. *Highway Performance Monitoring System—Reassessment.* Docket No. FHWA-2006-23638. Federal Highway Administration, U.S. Department of Transportation, Washington, D.C., April 10, 2006, http://edocket.access.gpo.gov/2006/E6-5139.htm. Accessed August 28, 2009.

73. *Highway Performance Monitoring System Reassessment Final Report.* Report FHWA-PL-99-001. Office of Highway Information Management, Federal Highway Administration, U.S. Department of Transportation, Washington, D.C., 1999, http://www.fhwa.dot.gov/ohim/fin_rpt.pdf. Accessed August 28, 2009.

74. *HPMS Reassessment 2010+ Data Specifications—Final Version.* Office of Highway Policy Information, Federal Highway Administration, U.S. Department of Transportation, Washington, D.C., May 2009, http://knowledge.fhwa.dot.gov/cops/hcx.nsf/All+Documents/F5157EFDC1A410B5852575C800500990/$FILE/HPMS%20Data%20Specifications%20Final.doc. Accessed August 28, 2009.

75. *Highway Performance Monitoring System (HPMS) Data Collection Field Manual.* Office of Highway Policy Information, Federal Highway Administration, U.S. Department of Transportation, Washington, D.C., 2009, http://knowledge.fhwa.dot.gov/cops/hcx.nsf/All+Documents/189DAE98F5722F7E852574FD0060AD4F/$FILE/2009%20Data%20Col%20Field%20Manual%20draft%2011-10.doc. Accessed August 28, 2009.

76. Source and Accuracy Compendium. Bureau of Transportation Statistics, Research and Innovative Technology Administration, Washington, D.C., undated. http://www.bts.gov/programs/statistical_policy_and_research/source_and_accuracy_compendium/. Accessed May 11, 2009.

77. *Highway Needs: An Evaluation of DOT's Process for Assessing the Nation's Highway Needs.* Report GAO/RCED-87-136, United States General Accounting Office, Washington, D.C., August 1987, http://www.gao.gov/products/RCED-87-136. Accessed August 28, 2009.

78. An Introduction to National Economic Accounting. Methodology Papers: U.S. National Income and Product Accounts. Bureau of Economic Analysis, U.S. Department of Commerce, Springfield, Virginia, March 1985. http://www.bea.gov/scb/pdf/NATIONAL/NIPA/Methpap/methpap1.pdf. Accessed May 11, 2009.

79. U.S. Economic Accounts. Bureau of Economic Analysis, U.S. Department of Commerce, Washington, D.C., undated. http://www.bea.gov/. Accessed May 11, 2009.

80. Concepts and Methods of the U.S. National Income and Product Accounts. Bureau of Economic Analysis, U.S. Department of Commerce, Washington, D.C., July 2008. http://www.bea.gov/national/pdf/NIPAhandbookch1-4.pdf. Accessed May 11, 2009.

81. All NIPA Tables. Bureau of Economic Analysis, U.S. Department of Commerce, Washington, D.C., undated. http://www.bea.gov/national/nipaweb/SelectTable.asp?Selected=N. Accessed August 31, 2009.

82. B. Fang and X. Han. Transportation Satellite Accounts: A New Way of Measuring Transportation Services in America. Report BTS99-R-01, Bureau of Transportation Statistics, Research and Innovative Technology Administration, Washington, D.C., February 1999. http://www.bts.gov/publications/transportation_satellite_accounts/. Accessed May 7, 2010.

83. *A Guide to the National Income and Product Accounts of the United States.* Bureau of Economic Analysis, U.S. Department of Commerce, Washington, D.C., undated. http://www.bea.gov/scb/pdf/misc/nipaguid.pdf. Accessed August 27, 2009.

84. Articles. National Economic Accounts. Bureau of Economic Analysis, U.S. Department of Commerce, Washington, D.C., 2009. http://www.bea.gov/national/an1.htm. Accessed August 27, 2009.

85. E. Seskin and S. Smith. *Preview of the 2009 Comprehensive Revision of the NIPAs—Changes in Definitions and Presentations.* Bureau of Economic Analysis, U.S. Department of Commerce, Washington, D.C., 2009. http://www.bea.gov/scb/pdf/2009/03%20March/0309_nipa_preview.pdf. Accessed August 29, 2009.

86. Updated Security and Release Procedures. Memorandum. Bureau of Economic Analysis, U.S. Department of Commerce, Washington, D.C., 2002. http://www.bea.gov/about/pdf/security-release-procedures.pdf. Accessed August 28, 2009.

87. National ITS Architecture Version 6.0. U.S. Department of Transportation, Washington, D.C., January 2008. http://www.iteris.com/itsarch/index.htm. Accessed November 2, 2008.

88. National ITS Architecture Logical Architecture—Volume I Description. Research and Innovative Technology Administration, U.S. Department of Transportation, Washington D.C., May 2007. http://www.iteris.com/itsarch/html/menu/documents.htm. Accessed May 11, 2009.

89. List of ITS Standards by Development Status. Research and Innovative Technology Administration, Washington, D.C., August 20, 2009. http://www.standards.its.dot.gov/status.asp. Accessed August 20, 2009.

90. Intelligent Transportation Systems. Research and Innovative Technology Administration, U.S. Department of Transportation, Washington, D.C., undated. http://www.its.dot.gov/about.htm. Accessed May 11, 2009.

91. Workshop on Intelligent Vehicle/Highway Systems. Mobility 2000, San Antonio, Texas, February 15–17, 1989.

92. National Workshop on IVHS. Mobility 2000, San Antonio, Texas, March 19–21, 1990.

93. *Smart Highways. An Assessment of Their Potential to Improve Travel.* Report GAO/PEMD-91-18. U.S. General Accounting Office, Washington, D.C., May 1991. http://archive.gao.gov/d20t9/144029.pdf. Accessed August 17, 2009.

94. *Special Report 232: Advanced Vehicle and Highway Technologies.* Transportation Research Board, National Research Council, Washington, D.C., 1991.

95. *Transportation Infrastructure. Benefits of Traffic Control Signal Systems Are Not Being Fully Realized.* Report GAO/RCED-94-105. U.S. General Accounting Office, Washington, D.C., March 1994. http://archive.gao.gov/t2pbat3/151498.pdf. Accessed August 17, 2009.

96. *Smart Highways. Challenges Facing DOT's Intelligent Vehicle Highway Systems Program.* Report GAO/T-RCED-94-253. U.S. General Accounting Office, Washington, D.C., June 1994. http://archive.gao.gov/t2pbat3/151999.pdf. Accessed August 17, 2009.

97. G. Euler and H. D. Robertson. National ITS Program Plan. Synopsis. U.S. Department of Transportation, ITS America, Washington, D.C., March 1995. http://www.itsdocs.fhwa.dot.gov/jpodocs/repts_pr/3845.pdf. Accessed August 31, 2009.

98. *Surface Transportation. Reorganization, Program Restructuring, and Budget Issues.* Report GAO/T-RCED-95-103. U.S. General Accounting Office, Washington, D.C., February 1995. http://archive.gao.gov/t2pbat2/153480.pdf. Accessed August 17, 2009.

99. *Surface Transportation. Research Funding, Federal Role, and Emerging Issues.* Report GAO/RCED-96-233. U.S. General Accounting Office, Washington, D.C., September 1996. http://www.gao.gov/archive/1996/rc96233.pdf. Accessed August 17, 2009.

100. *Urban Transportation. Challenges to Widespread Deployment of Intelligent Transportation Systems.* Report GAO/RCED-97-74. U.S. General Accounting Office, Washington, D.C., February 1997. http://www.gao.gov/archive/1997/rc97074.pdf. Accessed August 17, 2009.

101. *DOT's Budget. Management and Performance Issues Facing the Department in Fiscal Year 1999.* Report GAO/T-RCED/AIMD-98-76. U.S. General Accounting Office, Washington, D.C., February 1998. http://www.gao.gov/archive/1998/r198076t.pdf. Accessed August 17, 2009.

102. *Intelligent Transportation Systems (ITS) Projects Book.* Intelligent Transportation Systems (ITS) Joint Program office, U.S. Department of Transportation, Washington, D.C., January 2002.

103. 23 CFR 940.9. Regional ITS architecture. http://ecfr.gpoaccess.gov/cgi/t/text/text-idx?c=ecfr&sid=f3136244f528a0f781bef116d8e71a77&rgn=div8&view=text&node=23:1.0.1.11.51.0.1.5&idno=23. Accessed December 9, 2009.

104. *Highway Congestion. Intelligent Transportation Systems' Promise for Managing Congestion Falls Short, and DOT Could Better Facilitate their Strategic Use.* Report GAO-05-943. U.S. Government Accountability Office, Washington, D.C., September 2005. http://www.gao.gov/new.items/d05943.pdf. Accessed August 17, 2009.

105. Standard Specification for Archiving ITS-Generated Traffic Monitoring Data. Standard E 2665, ASTM International, 2008.

106. National Spatial Data Infrastructure. Federal Geographic Data Committee, Washington, D.C., undated. http://www.fgdc.gov/nsdi/nsdi.html. Accessed May 29, 2009.

107. *Framework Introduction and Guide.* Federal Geographic Data Committee, U.S. Geological Survey, Reston, Virginia, undated. http://www.fgdc.gov/framework/handbook. Accessed September 7, 2009.

108. geodata.gov. Geospatial One-Stop, U.S. Geological Survey, Reston, Virginia, undated. http://gos2.geodata.gov/wps/portal/gos. Accessed September 8, 2009.

109. *Beyond Mapping: Meeting National Needs through Enhanced Geographic Information Science.* Mapping Science Committee, National Research Council, National Academies Press, Washington, D.C., 2006. http://www.nap.edu/catalog.php?record_id=11687. Accessed September 2, 2009.

110. *Geospatial Information: Better Coordination Needed to Identify and Reduce Duplicative Investments.* Report GAO-04-703, United States General Accounting Office, Washington, D.C., June 2004. http://www.gao.gov/new.items/d04703.pdf. Accessed September 2, 2009.

111. *The 1994 Plan for the National Spatial Data Infrastructure: Building the Foundation of an Information Based Society.* Federal Geographic Data Committee, Reston, Virginia, March 1994. http://www.fgdc.gov/policyandplanning/NSDI%20Strategy%201994.pdf. Accessed September 2, 2009.

112. A Strategy for the NSDI. Federal Geographic Data Committee, Reston, VA, 1997. http://www.fgdc.gov/policyandplanning/A%20Strategy%20for%20the%20NSDI%201997.doc. Accessed September 2, 2009.

113. Circular No. A-16 Revised. Office of Management and Budget, Washington, D.C., August 2002. http://www.whitehouse.gov/omb/rewrite/Circulars/a016/a016_rev.html. Accessed September 2, 2009.

86

114. *NSDI Future Directions Initiative: Towards a National Geospatial Strategy and Implementation Plan.* Final Report Federal Geographic Data Committee, Reston, Virginia, June 2004. http://www.fgdc.gov/policyandplanning/future-directions/reports/FD_Final_Report.pdf. Accessed September 2, 2009.

115. Geospatial Line of Business: Program Management Plan. Office of Management and Budget, Washington, D.C., March 24, 2008. http://www.fgdc.gov/geospatial-lob/PMP-redacted-June2008.pdf. Accessed September 2, 2009.

116. I. DeLoatch. The U.S. Federal Geographic Data Committee (FGDC) Story. In Proceedings of the Global Spatial Data Infrastructure Association 11 World Conference, Rotterdam, The Netherlands, June 16, 2009. http://www.gsdi.org/gsdi11/slides/tues/1.1d.pdf. Accessed September 2, 2009.

117. L. Koontz. *Geographic Information Systems: Challenges to Effective Data Sharing.* Report GAO-03-874T. United States General Accounting Office, Washington, D.C., June 2003. http://www.gao.gov/new.items/d03874t.pdf. Accessed September 2, 2009.

118. *A Strategic Framework for the National Spatial Data Infrastructure.* National States Geographic Information Council, Bel Air, Maryland, May 2009. http://www.nsgic.org/resources/strategic_framework_NSDI_NSGIC.pdf. Accessed September 2, 2009.

119. National Transportation Atlas Database. Bureau of Transportation Statistics, Research and Innovative Technology Administration, Washington, D.C., 2009. http://www.bts.gov/publications/national_transportation_atlas_database/2009. Accessed August 24, 2009.

120. K. Hancock. Spatial Data and Geographic Information Systems within the Bureau of Transportation Statistics. Center for Transportation Analysis, Oak Ridge National Laboratory, Bureau of Transportation Statistics, October 1994. http://ntl.bts.gov/DOCS/sdg.html. Accessed August 24, 2009.

121. North American Transportation Atlas Data (NORTAD) CD (DOS and Unix). Bureau of Transportation Statistics, Research and Innovative Technology Administration, Washington, D.C., 1998. http://www.bts.gov/publications/north_american_transportation_atlas_data/. Accessed August 25, 2009.

122. R. Wright, S. Lewis, and P. Solano. Welcome to BTS National Transportation Atlas Database (NTAD). 24th Annual ESRI International User Conference, San Diego, California, August 9–13, 2004. http://proceedings.esri.com/library/userconf/proc04/docs/pap1939.pdf. Accessed August 25, 2009.

123. Geographic Information. Bureau of Transportation Statistics, Research and Innovative Technology Administration, Washington, D.C., undated. http://www.bts.gov/programs/geographic_information_services/. Accessed August 27, 2009.

124. An overview of the geodatabase. ArcGIS Desktop 9.3 Help, Environmental Systems Research Institute, Redlands, California, July 2009. http://webhelp.esri.com/arcgisdesktop/9.3/index.cfm?TopicName=An_overview_of_the_geodatabase. Accessed August 31, 2009.

125. Freight Data for State Transportation Agencies. A Peer Exchange, Boston, Massachusetts, July 2005. Transportation Research Circular E-C080, Transportation Research Board, Washington, D.C., November 2005. http://freight.transportation.org/doc/freight/circular_freight.pdf. Accessed September 9, 2009.

126. Description of Transportation Data to be Collected for NYMTC's Products, Reports, and Performance Measures. New York Metropolitan Transportation Council, New York, New York, 2005. http://www.nymtc.org/data_services/Data%20coordination%20files/Data%20Items%20descriptions05-31-2005-PFAC.pdf. Accessed September 10, 2009.

127. Meeting Freight Data Challenges. Workshop, Chicago, Illinois, July 2007. http://onlinepubs.trb.org/onlinepubs/archive/conferences/2007/FreightData/FreightData.pdf. Accessed December 7, 2009.

128. North American Freight Flows Conference: Understanding Changes and Improving Data Sources. Irvine, California, 2009.

129. NCFRP Project 3, "Performance Measures for Freight Transportation." Transportation Research Board, National Academy of Sciences, Washington, D.C., 2009. http://www.trb.org/TRBNet/ProjectDisplay.asp?ProjectID=1575. Accessed May 11, 2009.

130. CEFM Documents. Electronic Freight Management, U.S. Department of Transportation, Washington, D.C., undated. http://projects.battelle.org/fih/Documents.htm. Accessed May 11, 2009.

131. *Guide to Good Statistical Practice in the Transportation Field.* Bureau of Transportation Statistics, Research and Innovative Technology Administration, Washington, D.C., May 2003. http://www.bts.gov/publications/guide_to_good_statistical_practice_in_the_transportation_field/. Accessed May 11, 2009.

132. NCFRP Project 20, "Guidebook for Developing Sub-national Commodity Flow Data." Transportation Research Board, Washington, D.C., 2009. http://144.171.11.40/cmsfeed/TRBNetProjectDisplay.asp?ProjectID=2663. Accessed September 10, 2009.

133. Guidelines for Ensuring and Maximizing the Quality, Objectivity, Utility, and Integrity of Information Disseminated by Federal Agencies. Office of Management and Budget, Washington, D.C., October 2001. http://www.whitehouse.gov/omb/fedreg/final_information_quality_guidelines.html. Accessed May 11, 2009.

134. *BTS Statistical Standards Manual.* Bureau of Transportation Statistics, Research and Innovative Technology Administration, Washington, D.C., October 2005. http://www.bts.gov/programs/statistical_policy_and_research/bts_statistical_standards_manual/index.html. Accessed May 11, 2009.

135. E-Government Act of 2002. Public Law 107-347, 107th Congress, Washington, D.C., December 2002. http://frwebgate.access.gpo.gov/cgi-bin/getdoc.cgi?dbname=107_cong_public_laws&docid=f:publ347.107.pdf. Accessed May 11, 2009.

136. DOT Privacy Impact Assessments (PIA). U.S. Department of Transportation, Washington, D.C., May 2009. http://www.dot.gov/pia.html. Accessed May 11, 2009.

137. TranStats. Bureau of Transportation Statistics, Research and Innovative Technology Administration, Washington, D.C., undated. http://www.transtats.bts.gov/. Accessed May 29, 2009.

138. *Understanding Metadata.* National Information Standards Organization, Bethesda, Maryland, 2004. http://www.niso.org/publications/press/UnderstandingMetadata.pdf. Accessed May 29, 2009.

139. Metadata Encoding and Transmission Standard. The Library of Congress, Washington, D.C., April 2009. http://www.loc.gov/standards/mets/. Accessed May 29, 2009.

140. *Systems Engineering for Intelligent Transportation Systems.* Federal Highway Administration, Washington, D.C., January 2007. http://ops.fhwa.dot.gov/publications/seitsguide/index.htm. Accessed May 29, 2009.

141. *Departmental Information Resource Management Manual (DIRMM).* U.S. Department of Transportation, Washington, D.C., undated. http://cio.ost.dot.gov/portal/site/cio/dirmm/index.html. Accessed May 29, 2009.

142. Dictionary. Bureau of Transportation Statistics, Research and Innovative Technology Administration, Washington, D.C., undated. http://www.bts.gov/dictionary/index.xml. Accessed May 29, 2009.

143. Definitions. 2007 Economic Census, U.S. Census Bureau, Washington, D.C., May 2009. http://www.census.gov/econ/census07/www/definitions/index.html. Accessed May 29, 2009.

144. Glossary. Energy Information Administration, Washington, D.C., undated. http://www.eia.doe.gov/glossary/index.html. Accessed May 29, 2009.

145. Intermodal Industry Reports. Intermodal Association of North America, Calverton, Maryland, 2009. http://www.intermodal.org/statistics_files/reports.shtml#ETSO. Accessed May 11, 2009.

146. Market News and Transportation Data. Agricultural Marketing Service, U.S. Department of Agriculture, Washington, D.C., 2008. http://www.ams.usda.gov/AMSv1.0/ams.fetchTemplateData.do?template=TemplateA&navID=MarketNewsAndTransportationData&leftNav=MarketNewsAndTransportationData&page=MarketNewsAndTransportationData&acct=AMSPW. Accessed May 11, 2009.

147. Form 41, Schedules T100 and T100(f) Air Carrier Data. Bureau of Transportation Statistics, Research and Innovative Technology Administration, Washington, D.C., undated. http://www.bts.gov/programs/statistical_policy_and_research/source_and_accuracy_compendium/form41_schedule.html. Accessed May 11, 2009.

148. Automated Commercial System. U.S. Customs and Border Protection, Washington, D.C., March 2003. http://www.cbp.gov/ImageCache/cgov/content/publications/yesyoucan_2epdf/v1/yesyoucan.pdf. Accessed May 11, 2009.

149. D. Berreth. Enterprise Data Warehouse: Where if Stands, Where it's Heading. U.S. Customs Today, U.S. Customs Service, Washington, D.C., August 2000. http://www.cbp.gov/custoday/aug2000/dwartic4.htm. Accessed May 20, 2009.

150. Automated Export System (AES). U.S. Customs and Border Protection, U.S. Department of Homeland Security, Washington, D.C., undated. http://www.cbp.gov/xp/cgov/trade/automated/aes/. Accessed May 11, 2009.

151. Bureau of Labor Statistics. U.S. Department of Labor, Washington, D.C., undated. http://www.bls.gov/data/. Accessed May 29, 2009.

152. Publications. Bureau of Transportation Statistics, Research and Innovative Technology Administration, Washington, D.C., undated. http://www.bts.gov/publications/. Accessed May 11, 2009.

153. Table A. Summary National Income and Product Accounts, 2007. Bureau of Economic Analysis, U.S. Department of Commerce, Washington, D.C., August 2008. http://www.bea.gov/scb/pdf/2008/08%20August/NIPA%20Tables/0808nipas_summary.pdf. Accessed August 31, 2009.

154. Business and Industry. Census Bureau Economic Programs. U.S. Census Bureau, Washington, D.C., April 2009. http://www.census.gov/econ/www/index.html. Accessed May 29, 2009.

155. *2007 Economic Census User Guide.* U.S. Census Bureau, Washington, D.C., March 2009. http://www.census.gov/econ/census07/pdf/econ_user_guide.pdf. Accessed May 29, 2009.

156. Vehicle Inventory and Use Survey—Discontinued. U.S. Census Bureau, Washington, D.C., September 2006. http://www.census.gov/svsd/www/vius/products.html. Accessed May 11, 2009.

157. *History of the 1997 Economic Census.* Publication POL/00–HEC. U.S. Census Bureau, Economics and Statistics Administration, July 2000. http://www.census.gov/prod/ec97/pol00-hec.pdf. Accessed May 11, 2009.

158. EIA. Energy Information Administration, U.S. Department of Energy, Washington, D.C., undated. http://www.eia.doe.gov/. Accessed May 11, 2009.

159. Search Results. Energy Information Administration, U.S. Department of Energy, Washington, D.C., undated. http://tonto.eia.doe.gov/bookshelf/SearchResults.asp?title=&product=&submit2=A-Z%2BList%2Bof%2Bpublications. Accessed May 11, 2009.

160. Fatality Analysis Reporting System. National Center for Statistics and Analysis, National Highway Traffic Safety Administration, Washington, D.C., undated. http://www.nhtsa.dot.gov/people/ncsa/fars.html. Accessed May 11, 2009.

161. J. Tessmer. *FARS Analytic Reference Guide 1975 to 2006.* National Highway Traffic Safety Administration, Washington, D.C., September 2006. ftp://ftp.nhtsa.dot.gov/FARS/FARS-DOC/USERGUIDE-2006.pdf. Accessed May 11, 2009.

162. *FARS Coding and Validation Manual.* National Highway Traffic Safety Administration, Washington, D.C., 2009. ftp://ftp.nhtsa.dot.gov/FARS/FARS-DOC/. Accessed May 11, 2009.

163. *Highway Safety. Further Opportunities Exist to Improve Data on Crashes Involving Commercial Motor Vehicles.* Report GAO-06-102, U.S. Government Accountability Office, Washington, D.C., November 2005. http://www.gao.gov/new.items/d06102.pdf. Accessed May 11, 2009.

164. FERC Annual Reports. Federal Energy Regulatory Commission, Washington, D.C., 2009. http://www.ferc.gov/about/strat-docs/annual_rep.asp. Accessed May 11, 2009.

165. *Fisheries of the United States—2002.* Office of Science and Technology, National Oceanic and Atmospheric Association, Washington, D.C., September 2003. http://www.st.nmfs.noaa.gov/st1/fus/current/. Accessed May 11, 2009.

166. The Census of Agriculture. National Agricultural Statistics Service, U.S. Department of Agriculture, Washington, D.C., 2009. http://www.agcensus.usda.gov/. Accessed May 11, 2009.

167. County Business Patterns. U.S. Bureau of the Census, Washington, D.C., 2008. http://www.census.gov/econ/cbp/index.html. Accessed May 11, 2009.

168. R. Curlee. Freight Demand Modeling: State of the Practice within Federal Agencies. TRB Conference on Freight Demand Modeling Tools for Public-Sector Decision Making, Washington, D.C., September 2006. http://onlinepubs.trb.org/onlinepubs/archive/conferences/2006/fdm/curlee.pdf. Accessed September 4, 2009.

169. Digital Metadata for FAF Release. Office of Freight Management and Operations, Federal Highway Administration, Washington, D.C., January 2008. http://www.ops.fhwa.dot.gov/freight/freight_analysis/faf/faf2hwytrk_2002_2035/networkdata/metadata.htm. Accessed May 11, 2009.

170. Privacy Impact Assessment. Hazardous Materials Information System (HMIS). Pipeline and Hazardous Materials Safety Administration, Washington, D.C., March 2006. http://www.dot.gov/pia/phmsa_hmis.htm. Accessed May 11, 2009.

171. Office of Hazardous Materials Safety. Pipeline and Hazardous Materials Safety Administration, Washington, D.C., undated. http://www.phmsa.dot.gov/hazmat. Accessed May 11, 2009.

172. 49 CFR 171. General Information, Regulations, and Definitions. http://ecfr.gpoaccess.gov/cgi/t/text/text-idx?c=ecfr&sid=21f285e1c11de01179caa60d43cccc67&rgn=div5&view=text&node=49:2.1.1.3.6&idno=49. Accessed May 28, 2009.

173. 49 CFR 191. Transportation of Natural and Other Gas by Pipeline; Annual Reports; Incident Reports, and Safety-Related Condition Reports. http://ecfr.gpoaccess.gov/cgi/t/text/text-idx?c=ecfr&sid=edb31ca0a51224e2b8a8bb426d7b0be8&rgn=div5&view=text&node=49:3.1.1.1.3&idno=49. Accessed May 28, 2009.

174. *Highway Performance Monitoring System—Data Dictionary.* Bureau of Transportation Statistics, Research and Innovative Technology Administration, Washington, D.C., 2007. http://www.bts.gov/publications/national_transportation_atlas_database/2007/html/hpms.html. Accessed February 15, 2008.

175. *Traffic Monitoring Guide.* Office of Highway Policy Information, Federal Highway Administration, Washington, D.C. May 2001. http://www.fhwa.dot.gov/ohim/tmguide/. Accessed May 11, 2009.

88

176. 49 CFR 369. Reports of Motor Carriers. http://ecfr.gpoaccess.gov/cgi/t/text/text-idx?c=ecfr&sid=62bfe0e80e6c834dbbbfc669900322aa&rgn=div5&view=text&node=49:5.1.1.2.12&idno=49. Accessed May 28, 2009.

177. Carrier Financial and Operating Statistics Information for Filers. Federal Motor Safety Carrier Administration, Washington, D.C., undated. http://www.fmcsa.dot.gov/forms/reporting/mcs_info.htm#fos. Accessed May 11, 2009.

178. Products and Reports: Motor Carriers of Property. Federal Motor Safety Carrier Administration, Washington, D.C., undated. http://www.fmcsa.dot.gov/forms/reporting/prod.htm. Accessed May 11, 2009.

179. Data Profile: Motor Carrier Financial & Operating Information. Bureau of Transportation Statistics, Research and Innovative Technology Administration, Washington, D.C., undated. http://www.transtats.bts.gov/DatabaseInfo.asp?DB_ID=170&Link=0. Accessed May 11, 2009.

180. Motor Carrier Management Information System. Federal Motor Safety Carrier Administration, Washington, D.C., 2006. http://mcmiscatalog.fmcsa.dot.gov/beta/Catalogs&Documentation/. Accessed May 11, 2009.

181. *Privacy Impact Assessment. Motor Carrier Management Information System (MCMIS)*. Federal Motor Carrier Safety Administration, Washington, D.C., December 2003. http://www.dot.gov/pia/fmcsa_mcmis.htm. Accessed May 11, 2009.

182. SafeStat Online. Federal Motor Safety Carrier Administration, Washington, D.C., 2009. http://ai.fmcsa.dot.gov/SafeStat/SafeStatMain.asp Accessed May 11, 2009.

183. SafeStat. Motor Carrier Safety Status Measurement System. Methodology: Version 8.6. Federal Motor Safety Carrier Administration, Washington, D.C., January 2004. http://ai.fmcsa.dot.gov/CarrierResearchResults/PDFs/SafeStat_method.pdf. Accessed May 11, 2009.

184. National Automotive Sampling System (NASS). National Highway Traffic Safety Administration, Washington, D.C., undated. http://www.nhtsa.dot.gov/portal/site/nhtsa/menuitem.331a23559ab04dd24ec86e10dba046a0/. Accessed May 11, 2009.

185. The National Hazardous Materials Route Registry. Federal Motor Carrier Safety Administration, Washington, D.C., undated. http://hazmat.fmcsa.dot.gov/nhmrr/index.asp. Accessed May 11, 2009.

186. *National Pipeline Mapping System. Standards for Pipeline, Liquefied Natural Gas and Breakout Tank Farm Operator Submissions*. Pipeline and Hazardous Materials Safety Administration, Washington, D.C., February 2009. http://www.npms.phmsa.dot.gov/Documents/Operator_Standards.pdf. Accessed May 11, 2009.

187. NPMS Public Map Viewer. Pipeline and Hazardous Materials Safety Administration, Washington, D.C., February 2009. http://www.npms.phmsa.dot.gov/default.htm. Accessed May 11, 2009.

188. Metadata for NHPN version 2005.08. Federal Highway Administration, Washington, D.C., July 2007. http://www.fhwa.dot.gov/planning/nhpn/docs/metadata.html. Accessed May 11, 2009.

189. The National Highway System. Federal Highway Administration, Washington, D.C., July 2007. http://www.fhwa.dot.gov/planning/nhs/. Accessed May 11, 2009.

190. 23 CFR 650C. National Bridge Inspection Standards. http://ecfr.gpoaccess.gov/cgi/t/text/text-idx?c=ecfr&sid=cdb3c37b283816abd5544623c338b4ed&rgn=div5&view=text&node=23:1.0.1.7.29&idno=23. Accessed May 28, 2009.

191. National Bridge Inspection Standards (NBIS). Federal Highway Administration, Washington, D.C., April 2008. http://www.fhwa.dot.gov/Bridge/nbis.htm. Accessed May 28, 2009.

192. Navigation Data Center. U.S. Army Corps of Engineers, Alexandria, Virginia, March 2009. http://www.ndc.iwr.usace.army.mil/index.htm. Accessed May 11, 2009.

193. Marine Information for Safety and Law Enforcement (MISLE) System. Privacy Impact Assessment. U.S. Department of Homeland Security, Washington, D.C., September 2009. http://www.dhs.gov/xlibrary/assets/privacy/privacy_pia_uscg_misle.pdf. Accessed December 14, 2009.

194. North American Transborder Freight Data. Bureau of Transportation Statistics, Research and Innovative Technology Administration, Washington, D.C., undated. http://www.bts.gov/transborder/. Accessed May 11, 2009.

195. Welcome to the Service Annual Survey. U.S. Census Bureau, Washington, D.C., March 2009. http://www.census.gov/econ/www/servmenu.html. Accessed May 11, 2009.

196. Historical Services Statistics: Historical Data. U.S. Census Bureau, Washington, D.C., January 25, 2007. http://www.census.gov/svsd/www/services/sas/sas_data/sashist.htm. Accessed December 3, 2008.

197. Statistics Canada, Ottawa, Ontario, May 2009. http://www.statcan.gc.ca/start-debut-eng.html. Accessed May 11, 2009.

198. Surveys and statistical programs by subject. Statistics Canada, Ottawa, Ontario, May 2009. http://www.statcan.gc.ca/imdb-bmdi/indext-eng.htm. Accessed May 11, 2009.

199. Industry Data > Economic Data. Surface Transportation Board, Washington, D.C., undated. http://www.stb.dot.gov/stb/index.html. Accessed May 29, 2009.

200. Class I Railroad Accounting and Financial Reporting—Transportation of Hazardous Materials. Advance Notice of Proposed RuleMaking. *Federal Register 74 (2)*. January 2009. http://www.setonresourcecenter.com/Register/2009/jan/05/248A.pdf. Accessed May 29, 2009.

201. TradeStats Express Home, Washington, D.C., undated. http://tse.export.gov/. Accessed May 11, 2009.

202. Foreign Trade Statistics. U.S. Census Bureau, Washington, D.C., 2008. http://www.census.gov/foreign-trade/www/. Accessed May 11, 2009.

203. Vehicle Travel Information System (VTRIS). Federal Highway Administration, Washington, D.C., September 2008. http://www.fhwa.dot.gov/ohim/ohimvtis.cfm. Accessed May 11, 2009.

204. Workforce Information Database. Analyst Resource Center, Des Moines, Iowa, undated. http://www.almisdb.org/19WIDatabase.cfm. Accessed May 11, 2009.

205. Publications. Association of American Railroads, 2009. http://pubs.aar.org/pubstores/. Accessed May 11, 2009.

206. Catalog. Association of American Railroads, 2009. http://pubs.aar.org/pubstores/listItems.aspx. Accessed May 11, 2009.

207. State of the Industry. American Trucking Associations, Arlington, Virginia, undated. http://www.truckline.com/Pages/Home.aspx. Accessed May 11, 2009.

208. Welcome to the Colography Group's Website. Colography Group, Atlanta, Georgia, October, 2006. http://www.colography.com/index.html. Accessed May 11, 2009.

209. IHS Global Insight, 2009. http://www.globalinsight.com/. Accessed May 11, 2009.

210. Uniform Intermodal Interchange and Facilities Access Agreement. Intermodal Association of North America, Calverton, Maryland, 2009. http://www.uiia.org/. Accessed May 11, 2009.

211. Lloyd's MIU, 2008. http://www.lloydsmiu.com/lmiu/index.htm. Accessed May 11, 2009.

212. Our Businesses. United Business Media Limited, undated. http://www.unitedbusinessmedia.com/ubm/ourbusinesses/. Accessed May 11, 2009.

213. PIERS Global Intelligent Solutions, undated. http://www.piers.com/default.aspx. Accessed May 11, 2009.

214. UBM Global Trade, undated. http://www.ubmglobaltrade.com/index.asp. Accessed May 11, 2009.

215. *Executive Summary.* State of Logistics Report, Council of Supply Chain Management Professionals, Lombard, Illinois, 2008. http://cscmp.org/memberonly/state.asp. Accessed May 11, 2009.

216. Airports Council International, Geneve, Switzerland, 2008. http://www.aci.aero/cda/aci_common/display/main/aci_content07_banners.jsp?zn=aci&cp=1_725_2___. Accessed May 11, 2009.

217. Border Information Flow Architecture. Federal Highway Administration, U.S. Department of Transportation, Washington D.C., January 2009. http://ops.fhwa.dot.gov/freight/freight_analysis/gateways_borders/freight_info/borderinfo/border.htm. Accessed May 11, 2009.

218. C. T. Lawson. Freight Informatics: 21st-Century Data Just in Time, *ITE Journal,* Institute of Transportation Engineers, December 2004, Vol. 74, No. 12, pp. 38–41.

219. Commercial Vehicle Information Systems and Networks (CVISN). Federal Motor Carrier Safety Administration, Washington, D.C., undated. http://www.fmcsa.dot.gov/facts-research/cvisn/index.htm. Accessed May 27, 2009.

220. *Commercial Vehicle Information Systems and Networks (CVISN) Architecture.* Publication POR-02-7364 V3.0. Federal Motor Carrier Safety Administration, Washington, D.C., December 2006. http://www.fmcsa.dot.gov/documents/cvisn/architecture/CVISN-Architecture-v3.pdf. Accessed May 27, 2009.

221. *Commercial Vehicle Information Systems and Networks (CVISN) Operational and Architectural Compatibility Handbook (COACH). Part 1. Operational Concept and Top-Level Design Checklists.* Publication NSTD-08-487 V4.0. Federal Motor Carrier Safety Administration, Washington, D.C., November 2008. http://www.fmcsa.dot.gov/documents/cvisn/architecture/COACH-pt1-v4.pdf. Accessed May 27, 2009.

222. FGDC-endorsed standards. Federal Geographic Data Committee, Washington, D.C., 1998. http://www.fgdc.gov/standards/projects/FGDC-standards-projects/fgdc-endorsed-standards. Accessed September 9, 2009.

223. S. Shin, B. Westcott, and L. Wayne. Making the Transition to International Metadata. *Proceedings of the 45th Annual Conference of the Urban and Regional Information Systems Association,* Washington, D.C., August 20, 2007. http://www.fgdc.gov/library/presentations/documents/URISA_Metadata_2007.pdf. Accessed September 2, 2009.

224. Electronic Freight Management. Intelligent Transportation Systems, Research and Innovative Technology Administration, Washington, D.C., undated. http://www.its.dot.gov/efm/index.htm. Accessed May 11, 2009.

225. M. Jensen, M. Williamson, R. Sanchez, and C. Mitchell. *Electronic Intermodal Supply Chain Manifest Field Operational Test Evaluation Draft Report.* ITS Joint Program Office, U.S. Department of Transportation, Washington, D.C., December 2002. http://www.itsdocs.fhwa.dot.gov/JPODOCS/REPTS_TE/13769.html. Accessed May 11, 2009.

226. D. Fitzpatrick, D. Dreyfus, M. Onder, and J. Sedor. *The Electronic Freight Management Initiative.* Report FHWA-HOP-06-085, Federal Highway Administration, Washington, D.C., April 2006. http://www.itsdocs.fhwa.dot.gov/JPODOCS/REPTS_TE/14246_files/14246.pdf. Accessed May 11, 2009.

227. R. Butler. Electronic Freight Management (EFM) & Cross-Town Improvement Project (C-TIP). Office of Freight Management and Operations, Federal Highway Administration, Washington, D.C., September 2009.

228. Performance Measurement. Office of Freight Management and Operations, Federal Highway Administration, Washington, D.C., October 2009. http://ops.fhwa.dot.gov/freight/freight_analysis/perform_meas/index.htm. Accessed December 10, 2009.

229. W. Mallett, C. Jones, J. Sedor, and J. Short. *Freight Performance Measurement: Travel Time in Freight-Significant Corridors.* Report FHWA-HOP-07-071, Office of Freight Management and Operations, Federal Highway Administration, Washington, D.C., December 2006. http://www.ops.fhwa.dot.gov/freight/freight_analysis/perform_meas/fpmtraveltime/traveltimebrochure.pdf. Accessed May 11, 2009.

230. J. Short, R. Pickett, and J. Christianson. *Freight Performance Measures Analysis of 30 Freight Bottlenecks.* American Transportation Research Institute, Arlington, Virginia, March 2009, 228 pp.

231. R. Tardif. Freight Data Partnerships and Products. Providing Ongoing Commercial Vehicle Data from GPS Providers. Presentation at the *North American Freight Flows Conference: Understanding Changes and Improving Data Sources.* Irvine, California, 2009.

232. *Continental Gateway Road Network Performance.* Draft Interim Report—Border Crossings and Intermodal Terminals. Transport Canada, March 2009.

233. A. Carter. Multimodal Hazmat Intelligence Portal (HIP). COHMED Conference, Mesa, Arizona, January 2009. www.cvsa.org/programs/documents/cohmed/COHMED2009/HIP%20Presentation.ppt. Accessed May 11, 2009.

234. FY 2007 E-Government Act Report. U.S. Department of Transportation, Washington, D.C., undated. http://www.dot.gov/webpoliciesnotices/dotegovactreport2007.htm. Accessed May 11, 2009.

DEFINITION OF TERMS

Architecture. An architecture is the organizational structure of a system, identifying its components, their interfaces, and a concept of execution among them.

Bill of lading. A bill of lading is a receipt given by a carrier to the shipper acknowledging receipt of the goods to be transported.

Business process model. A business process model is a representation of processes. A variety of tools and techniques may be used depending on the specific need, including flow charts, Gantt charts, project evaluation and review technique (PERT) charts, integration definition (IDEF) methods, and business process modeling notation (BPMN).

Commodity. Different definitions exist. A common definition is that commodity is a product that can be bought and sold. Another commonly used definition is that a commodity is a product for which there is demand but is supplied without differentiation.

Conceptual model. A conceptual data model is a representation of concepts and their relationships. As such, conceptual data models provide a mapping of relationships and rules (e.g., hazardous materials can only be routed on certain corridors) that facilitate the understanding and implementation of logical and physical data models.

Container. A container is a device that holds or encloses objects to facilitate their movement. A specific type of container is a shipping container.

Data architecture. Data architecture is the manner and process to organize and integrate data components. Data architectures usually include one or more of the following elements: business process model, conceptual model, logical model, physical model, and data dictionary.

Data dictionary. A data dictionary is a listing that contains definitions, characteristics, and other properties of entities, attributes, and other data elements. An alternative (or complement) to a data dictionary is a metadata document.

Data model. A data model is an abstract representation of data characteristics and relationships. Examples of data models include business process models, conceptual data models, logical data models, and physical data models.

Database. A database is a structured collection of records stored in a computer system. The structure of the records is documented by using physical data models.

Framework. A framework is a basic conceptual structure to address, analyze, and solve complex problems. By comparison, a software framework is a re-usable component of a software application.

Invoice. An invoice is an itemized list of goods with an account of the amount due to the seller.

Item. An item (or product) is an object included in a shipment.

Logical model. A logical data model is a representation of data characteristics and relationships at a level that is independent of any physical implementation.

Manifest. A manifest is a document that lists the contents in a shipment.

Metadata. Metadata (or "data about data") are generalizations of data dictionaries that contain structured information about data. Metadata documents are structured, normally following agreed upon standards, to facilitate information retrieval, use, and management. Examples of metadata standards at the federal level are CSDGM, which is maintained by FGDC, and METS, which is maintained by the Library of Congress. CSDGM became mandatory for federal agencies in January 1995. Nationwide, state and local agencies are increasingly adopting and using CSDGM, partly because of the availability of user-friendly CSDGM editors such as those included in commonly used GIS applications.

Mode of transportation. A mode of transportation is a term that describes a functional combination of vehicles, containers, transportation network, and traffic control. Different modes of transportation involve different combinations of vehicles, containers, transportation network, and traffic control. Common modes of freight transportation in the United States are air, rail, truck, pipeline, and water. Each of these modes of transportation can include subtypes.

Motor carrier. A motor carrier is an entity or an individual in the business of transporting goods by truck.

Physical model. A physical data model is a representation of data characteristics and relationships that depends on the specific physical platform chosen for its implementation. In the context of a national freight data architecture, physical models might be developed to illustrate sample applications of the logical model.

Product. See Item.

Purchase order. A purchase order is a document that conveys the intent to purchase items.

Shipment. A shipment is an identifiable collection of items or goods to be transported.

Shipper. A shipper is the sender of a shipment.

Specification. A specification is a set of requirements that a process, product, or service must meet. Common types of specifications in highway construction include method specifications, performance-based specifications, and performance-related specifications. Common types of specifications used for software applications include functional specifications and software requirement specifications.

Standard. A standard is an established reference norm or requirement, usually developed through a collective discussion and approval process. Standards can be developed by single organizations, trade groups, and standards organizations. Data standards are usually established by consensus and are approved by an accredited standards development organization.

System. A system is an integrated composite of people, products, and processes, which provide a capability to satisfy a stated need or objective.

Traffic control system. A traffic control system is the set of systems, protocols, and procedures that facilitate the safe movement of vehicles on a transportation network.

Transportation network. A transportation network is the set of physical elements where a vehicle moves and freight can be stored and/or processed. Examples of transportation network components include terminals, highway and rail segments, waterways, intersections, inspection facilities, rail classification yards, ports, land ports of entry warehousing facilities, cross dock facilities, and intermodal facilities.

Vehicle. A vehicle is a means of conveyance. A vehicle gives a container locomotion and mobility along a specific path. Depending on its physical characteristics, a vehicle could also provide containment.

Waybill. A waybill is a document issued by a carrier describing the origin, destination, route, and other relevant characteristics of the shipment.

ABBREVIATIONS, ACRONYMS, INITIALISMS, AND SYMBOLS

3PL	Third-party logistics
AADT	Annual average daily traffic
AAR	American Association of Railroads
AASHTO	American Association of State Highway and Transportation Officials
ABI	Automated Broker Interface
ACE	Automated Commercial Environment
ACI	Airports Council International
ACS	Automated Commercial System
ADUS	Archived data user service
AES	Automated Export System
AIS	Automatic identification system
ALMIS	America's Labor Market Information System
AMPO	Association of Metropolitan Planning Organizations
AMS	Automated Manifest System
ANSI ASC	American National Standards Institute Accredited Standards Committee
ARC	Analyst Resource Center
ARDIS	Airline Reporting and Data Information System
AS	Applicability Statement
ASCII	American Standard Code for Information Interchange
ASTM	American Society for Testing and Materials
ATA	American Trucking Associations
ATCS	Advanced Train Control Systems
ATIS	Advanced traveler information system
ATMS	Advanced traffic management system
ATN	Aeronautical Telecommunications Network
ATRI	American Transportation Research Institute
AVCS	Advanced vehicle control system
BEA	Bureau of Economic Analysis
BIFA	Border Information Flow Architecture
BIIF	Basic image interchange format
BLS	Bureau of Labor Statistics
BOL	Bill of lading
BPMN	Business process modeling notation
BTS	Bureau of Transportation Statistics
C&P	Condition and performance
C2C	Center-to-Center

CADD	Computer-aided design and drafting
CBD	Central business district
CBP	U.S. Customs and Border Protection
CBSA	Core-Based Statistical Area
CDS	Crashworthiness Data System
CEFM	Columbus Electronic Freight Management
CES	Current Employment Statistics
CFR	Code of Federal Regulations
CFS	Commodity Flow Survey
CICA	Context Inspired Component Architecture
CIREN	Crash Injury Research and Engineering Network
CITES	Convention on International Trade in Endangered Species
CMSPI	Couriers and Messengers Services Price Index
COACH	CVISN Operational and Architectural Compatibility Handbook
COFC	Container on flatcar
CPC	Central Product Classification
CPI	Consumer price index
CSCMP	Council of Supply Chain Management Professionals
CSDGM	Content Standard for Digital Geospatial Metadata
CV	Commercial vehicle
CVISN	Commercial Vehicle Information Systems and Networks
CVO	Commercial vehicle operations
DBMS	Database management system
DFD	Data flow diagram
DHS	Department of Homeland Security
DLG	Digital line graph
DOT	Department of transportation
DRIVE	Dedicated Road Infrastructure for Vehicle Safety
DSRC	Dedicated short-range communication
DVD	Digital video disk
ECM	Engine control module
EDI	Electronic data interchange
EDS	Electronic Data System
EDW	Enterprise data warehouse
EFM	Electronic freight management
EIA	Energy Information Administration
EMS	Engine control module
EPA	Environmental Protection Agency
ESCM	Electronic Supply Chain Manifest
ESRI	Environmental Systems Research Institute
FAA	Federal Aviation Administration
FACET	Future Automated Commercial Environment Team
FAF	Freight Analysis Framework
FAK	Freight-all-kinds
FARS	Fatality Analysis Reporting System

FAZ	Freight analysis zone
FDA	Food and Drug Administration
FERC	Federal Energy Regulatory Commission
FFA	Flow of Funds Accounts
FGDC	Federal Geographic Data Committee
FHWA	Federal Highway Administration
FICCDC	Federal Interagency Coordinating Committee on Digital Cartography
FIPS PUBS	Federal Information Processing Standards Publication
FMCSA	Federal Motor Carrier Safety Administration
FPM	Freight Performance Measurement
FRA	Federal Railroad Administration
FTA	Federal Transit Administration
FTS	Foreign Trade Statistics
GAO	Government Accountability Office
GDP	Gross domestic product
GDS	Global Distribution Systems
GES	General Estimates System
GIS	Geographic information system
GML	Geography Markup Language
GNP	Gross national product
GPS	Global Positioning System
Hazmat	Hazardous material
HIP	Hazmat Intelligence Portal
HIPAA	Health Insurance Portability and Accountability Act
HMIS	Hazardous Materials Information System
HOV	High-occupancy vehicle
HPMS	Highway Performance Monitoring System
HS	Harmonized System
HTS	Harmonized Tariff Schedule
HTTPS	Hypertext transfer protocol over secure socket layer
I-O	Input-Output
IANA	Intermodal Association of North America
IBET	Intermodal Bottleneck Evaluation Tool
IBM	International Business Machines
ICC	Interstate Commerce Commission
IDEF	Integration definition
IEEE	Institute of Electrical and Electronic Engineers
IFDS	International Freight Data System
IMT&S	Intermodal Market Trends & Statistics
INCITS	InterNational Committee for Information Technology Standards
IRI	International Roughness Index
IRS	Internal Revenue Service
ISIC	International Standard Industrial Classification
ISO	International Organization of Standards
ISTEA	Intermodal Surface Transportation Efficiency Act

ITDS	International Trade Data System
ITS	Intelligent transportation system
IVHS	Intelligent Vehicle/Highway System
JPO	Joint Program Office
LNG	Liquefied natural gas
LoB	Line of Business
LOS	Level of service
LPMS	Lock Performance Monitoring System
LRS	Linear Referencing System
LTCCS	Large Truck Crash Causation Study
LTL	Less-than-truckload
MA	Metropolitan area
MARAD	Maritime Administration
MCMIS	Motor Carrier Management Information System
MCSAP	Motor Carrier Safety Assistance Program
METS	Metadata Encoding and Transmission Standard
MFRS	Mileage Facilities Reporting System
MISLE	Marine Information for Safety and Law Enforcement
MPO	Metropolitan planning organization
MS/ETMCC	Message Sets for External Traffic Management Center Communications
MSA	Metropolitan statistical area
MXP	Import/Export Price Index
NAAQS	National ambient air quality standards
NAFTA	North American Free Trade Agreement
NAICS	North American Industry Classification System
NAPCS	North American Product Classification System
NASA	National Aeronautics and Space Administration
NASS	National Automotive Sampling System
NATAP	North American Trade Automation Prototype
NBI	National Bridge Inventory
NBIS	National Bridge Inspection Standards
NCFRP	National Cooperative Freight Research Program
NCHRP	National Cooperative Highway Research Program
NCSC	National Crosswalk Service Center
NDC	Navigation Data Center
NHMRR	National Hazardous Materials Route Registry
NHN	National Highway Network
NHPN	National Highway Planning Network
NHS	National Highway System
NHTSA	National Highway Traffic Safety Administration
NIPA	National Income and Product Accounts
NIST	National Institute of Standards and Technology
NITL	National Industrial Transportation League
NMFC	National motor freight classification
NMFTA	National Motor Freight Traffic Association

NMVCCS	National Motor Vehicle Crash Causation Study
NORTAD	North American Transportation Atlas Database
NPMS	National Pipeline Mapping System
NSDI	National Spatial Data Infrastructure
NST	Standards Nomenclature for Transport Statistics
NTAD	National Transportation Atlas Database
NTAR	National transportation analysis region
NTN	National Truck Network
NWN	National Waterway Network
NYMTC	New York Metropolitan Transportation Council
O-D	Origin-destination
OAI	Office of Airline Information
OASIS	Organization for the Advancement of Structured Information Standards
OMB	Office of Management and Budget
ORNL	Oak Ridge National Laboratory
OTII	Office of Trade and Industry Information
PERT	Project evaluation and review technique
PGA	Participating government agency
PHMSA	Pipeline and Hazardous Materials Safety Administration
PIA	Privacy impact assessment
PIERS	Port Import Export Reporting Service
PLU	Price look-up
PPI	Producer price index
QCEW	Quarterly Census of Employment and Wages
RCAF	Rail Cost Adjustment Factor
RITA	Research and Innovative Technology Administration
RLF	Remote Location Filing
S&P	Standard & Poor's
SaDIP	Safety Data Improvement Program
SAE	Society of Automotive Engineers
SafeStat	Motor Carrier Safety Status Measurement System
SAFETEA-LU	Safe, Accountable, Flexible, Efficient Transportation Equity Act: A Legacy for Users
SCI	Special Crash Investigations
SCOP	Standing Committee on Planning
SCTG	Standard Classification of Transported Goods
SDS	Standard dataset
SDTS	Spatial Data Transfer Standard
SEA	Safety evaluation area
SED	Shipper export declaration
SIC	Standard industrial classification
SITC	Standard International Trade Classification
SOAP	Simple object access protocol
SPLC	Standard point location code
SQL	Structured Query Language

STB	Surface Transportation Board
STCC	Standard transportation commodity code
STRACNET	Strategic Rail Corridor Network
STRAHNET	Strategic Highway Network
SUV	Sport utility vehicle
TCOD	Trucking Commodity Origin and Destination
TEA-21	Transportation Equity Act for the 21st Century
TECS	Treasury Enforcement Communications System
TIUS	Truck Inventory and Use Survey
TL	Truckload
TMC	Traffic management center
TMDD	Traffic Management Data Dictionary
TMG	Traffic Monitoring Guide
TMS	transportation management systems
TOFC	Trailer on flatcar
TRB	Transportation Research Board
TTCI	Transportation Technology Center, Inc.
TTI	Texas Transportation Institute
TxDOT	Texas Department of Transportation
UBL	Universal Business Language
UBM	United Business Media
UCR	Unified Carrier Registration
UIIA	Uniform Intermodal Interchange & Facilities Access Agreement
UN/EDIFACT	United Nations/Electronic Data Interchange for Administration, Commerce, and Transport
URCS	Uniform Railroad Costing System
USACE	U.S. Army Corps of Engineers
USC	U.S. Code
USCG	U.S. Coast Guard
USDA	U.S. Department of Agriculture
USGS	U.S. Geological Survey
USITC	U.S. International Trade Commission
VAN	Value-added network
VIUS	Vehicle Inventory and Use Survey
VMT	Vehicle miles traveled
VS/F	Volume/service flow
VTRIS	Vehicle Travel Information System
WCO	World Customs Organization
WCSC	Waterborne Commerce Statistics Center
WCUS	Waterborne Commerce of the United States
WID	Workforce Information Database
XML	Extensible markup language